STAINED-GLASS CRAFT

STAINED-

JACK W. BERNSTEIN

HISTORICAL PREFACE BY LEON GORDON MILLER

GLASS CRAFT

Macmillan Publishing Co., Inc.
New York

Collier Macmillan Publishers
London

Macmillan Publishing Co., Inc.
866 Third Avenue, New York, N.Y. 10022
Collier-Macmillan Canada Ltd., Toronto, Ontario

Library of Congress Catalog Card Number: 72-91258

First Printing

Printed in the United States of America

TO THOSE

WHO LIKE STAINED GLASS

CONTENTS

HISTORICAL

PREFACE

It is quite probable that the first glass on earth was created by natural forces when sand, potash, or soda ash were subjected to heat, then flowed and cooled into the vitreous form that we know as glass. Among the early tools used by man were arrowheads and cutting instruments of obsidian, a natural glass substance created through such a process.

While historians differ in their dating of the first man-made glass, this invention is assumed to have taken place about 3000 B.C. There is agreement that the phenomenon took place in the Middle East, where the oldest known sample of glass was found in the Euphrates region and is believed to have been made in 2500 B.C.

Early glass craft was practiced in Egypt many centuries prior to the Christian era, and Alexandria became the first world glass-producing center. While the earliest Egyptian glass is dated roughly about 1500 B.C., older samples of glass have been discovered in Egypt. It is assumed that these earlier pieces were imported from Syria. Nevertheless, the birth and development of the art of glassmaking is attributed to Egypt, and the earliest known factory at Tel el Amara in Egypt is believed to have been flourishing in 1400 B.C.

In Alexandria the glassmaker produced beads, amulets, and vessels. The glass had both translucence and color. In almost all cases the color resulted from impurities. The nature of the impurities and oxides determined the final result. Cobalt oxides produced blue. Chromic oxides produced red. Technical knowledge was limited and the successful repetition of colors depended upon the source of available materials.

As early as the sixth century B.C., under the reign of Ashurbanipal, a series of tablets described in detail the fabricating techniques of the process and depicted the materials that were used in the producing of glass. Most of the techniques in use centuries later already were known in this period of antiquity.

From the ancient eras into the periods of Greek and Roman domination, Egypt retained her position as the glass center of the world. It was from Egypt that the Greeks and Romans learned the craft, distributed glass products through trade, and disseminated the knowledge of glassmaking throughout their empires.

In the first century before Christianity the Romans established the art-craft of glassmaking within their borders, and during the life of the Roman Empire great strides were made in advancing glass technology. New forms in glass were perfected, new colors were introduced, and production techniques and design development reached a high point in the art. Through Rome's commerce in bottles, vases, beads, and other glass products, the medium was introduced to all parts of the Roman Empire, including faraway Gaul, Spain, and Northern Europe.

Although the ancient art of glassmaking became known in these areas of Europe, conditions were not ripe for the craft to flourish. Between the decline of ancient Rome and the emergence of Western Christendom came changes in both practice and spirit that would profoundly alter the direction of the development and use of glassmaking.

While the earliest structures of the Christian era began to incorporate glass into architecture, the pattern followed was that of the affluent Roman home. The first Church of St. Peter, built by Constantine in 326, contained rows of columns to define the nave, surrounded by support walls that provided at the top for clearstory windows to supply light into the nave.

The introduction of glass as an integral part of architecture was a brilliant and significant innovation in the mainstream of architectural history. Yet not until more centuries had passed were these clearstories to be transformed into the magnificent new art form which we identify as the stained-glass window.

Much earlier in Egypt a technique was employed that forecast later development of the stained-glass window. Pieces of colored glass were set into openings in buildings to color the light that came through. The technique was much the same as used with faceted glass today by contemporary glass designers who chip the slab or pot glass and insert the chunks with epoxy or cement into structural openings in a pre-planned design.

Inspired by the new spiritual philosophy of Christianity that took root under Constantine and prevailed during the centuries of the Byzantine Empire, all of the arts and crafts were put to the new and compelling purpose of enhancing the edifices and ceremonies that surrounded the Byzantine emperors.

During this time, as early as the fourth and fifth centuries, mosaics of glass were made for the Church. New color sources were discovered. Oxides of various types were introduced, gold to create ruby red, stannic cupric and silver to produce yellows and greens. New furnaces, iron tubes for blowing, forms for shaping, newly designed annealing ovens were made, and techniques became more varied for forming the glass.

Isolated by the rise of Islam to the East, a dying Rome, and still barbarian tribes to the west and north, Byzantium addressed itself to the perfecting of the ancient arts.

Details of these early centuries are sparse, but we know that the period that witnessed transformation of ancient Rome into the Rome of Christendom, also saw many visitations from the north. One who came in peace and who was crucial to the subsequent shaping of western civilization and the rise of high Christian art was Charlemagne, crowned as head of the Holy Roman Empire in Rome in 800 A.D. On his return home, Charlemagne visited Ravenna where Byzantine accomplishment so impressed him that he determined to reproduce the splendors of San Vitale, which held the mosaics of Justinian and Theodora, for his own palace chapel at Aachen.

In all important respects, the age of Charlemagne, who performed the remarkable feat of salvaging the early Christian heritage and commissioning its continuance through the work of many hundreds of scribes and artists, laid the foundation for the great era that would unfold, of Gothic art and architecture which gave birth to the new and spectacular art form of the stained-glass window.

In its traditional reference, stained glass is a pattern or mosaic cut of glass that is held together in a panel by lead strips, concrete, epoxy, or other linear means. The earliest reference to the technique is from ninth-century documents that refer to colored-glass windows in a church. In the tenth century there is a specific reference by the Bishop of Rheims to windows of a figurative design that told a story.

While there is controversy as to which are the oldest windows still in existence, many historians believe them to be the series of prophets at Augsburg Cathedral made in the eleventh century. Reference has also been made to a St. Benedictine monastery of this century in Monte Cassino that had a chapel filled with stained-glass windows.

The first account of artisans knowledgeable in the stained glassmaking craft declares that Venetian glassmakers settled in the village of Limoges in the year 959.

The skill required to practice stained glassmaking was sophisticated and carried with it much prestige. In Venice, center of both trade and artistic handicraft during the Byzantine era and later, serious penalties were attached to the disclosure of trade and craft secrets to persons who were not Venetians. But like all efforts to contain knowledge, this too failed, for stained glassmaking, like other skills, was more and more coming into demand by the emerging institutions of a waking Europe.

The knowledge of the stained glassmaking craft is believed to have entered Europe by two routes, the land route emanating north toward the regions of Germany and Austria, and the sea route from Venice, via Spain, which brought knowledge of the craft to France. All over Europe the stage was set for one of the most astonishing performances in architecture and the arts that the world has ever known.

Spanning a period that began in the ninth century and continued to the fifteenth century, the total environment—physical, theological, and esthetic—came under the patronage and discipline of the Christian Church. From this inspiration was created some of the most significant art in stained glass ever produced. The skills were of high level, objectives were clear, time for execution of projects was unlimited, and religious fervor was at its zenith.

Throughout the Middle Ages the arts were practiced as direct communications media. The intent was to convey through sculpture, stained glass, and in more intimate works in gold, enameling, and illuminated manuscript the religious stories of the Christian faith. The early windows had as their objective the communication to an illiterate populace of a familiarity with the personages and acts that constituted their religion.

The twelfth century is recognized today as a high point in ecclesiastic art, an era not only of great architecture and sculpture, but also of superlative gold and enamel work, vestments, and creations in stained glass; work of highest quality was produced for new churches and cathedrals all over Europe.

The stained glassmakers of this era did not strive for Naturalism. The glass became an integral part of the architecture. There was virtually no form in the drawing of the windows, but rather a flat pattern, frequently of many pieces of glass, telling a story, yet not representational. The intent was to create a luminosity within an area of darkness that would elicit an emotional response from the viewer. The luminous effect of the stained glass became an important decorative element of the interior, as well as an integral part of the architecture.

In these early days of stained-glass design, the cost of producing windows was so high that only institutions of immense wealth and importance could raise the funds to commission them. Only the churches and cathedrals were deemed adequately worthy during this period when the Church was the dominant authority, patron, and unifying agent over all human activity in Europe. The surge in religious architecture commanded the energies and funds of both rich and poor, the nobleman and the commoner alike. The entire populace sensed the birth of a new order in society, an order based on belief in God and an acceptance of the conviction that all aspects of life, all actions of man, all development of structure and systems was for, and existed through, the omnipotence of God. The Church was God's agent on earth and held the power to determine man's destiny.

It was within this all-pervasive atmosphere that the great art of the era was produced. As patron, the Church set the basic rules for creation of works of art, commissioned them, and accepted or rejected all design concepts. The Church encouraged the concept that all things in existence had relevance only as they reflected God. Art served to exalt God and became equated with the idea of God and Christ. This concept inspired higher and more majestic buildings, and as they reached higher, the enclosed space within required light and glass both to hold the scale and illuminate the interior of the structure.

A stained-glass style emerged that was suited to the architectural reality of the time. Despite St. Bernard's prohibition against use of the figurative element in stained glass, tall elongated figures were designed to accommodate the window areas of the high structures. Most glass designs were conceived as flat patterns. Figures were large and had large heads. They were emphasized by strong linear outlines that boldly delineated form. Drapery was parallel, angular, and emphasized by linear repeats.

In Italy, Duccio created for the Cathedral in Siena a series of windows that followed all the stylistic rules, even though they carry the identity of his personal manner of work. He added geometric, stylized borders with repeat patterns. In his windows, as in his paintings, he brings a powerful emotional impact that communicates to us in this century the importance of "God and the Church" to the populace of the period.

In the Church of St. Denis in an early surviving stained-glass window made for the Abbot Sugar we find an extension of the use of borders and panels designed in glass. The design seems to have been inspired by the then contemporary wrought iron work, possibly used as a border. Inasmuch as only a fragment survived the destruction of Church art during the French Revolution and the only reference is an early drawing, we must assume its placement. This type of detail is rare for the period, but there

Farbigem glass mural—World History of Medicine, Ohio State University Medical Center.

WORK OF WILLET STUDIOS

Flower form.

Window.

LEON GORDON MILLER

are a few others, such as the decorative border of the German Masters windows at Assisi. The chapels of a number of churches have small decorative windows combining roundels, geometric, leaf, and floral abstracts and are believed to have been commissioned in this design idiom primarily because it was much less expensive to make than thematic windows. Stylized foliage and floral designs were frequently used to fill corners and as backgrounds.

One of the first writers to describe how windows were made was Theophilus, who explained the use of paint and wine as colorants and thinners. The Cloisters Museum in New York City displays a panel from which the glass has been removed, making it possible to study the leading and the part it played in design. The window, called *Flagellation,* reveals that the leading not only separates the colors but becomes the basic, linear design. During the second world war, many stained-glass windows were removed to secure them against damage. This afforded students the opportunity to analyze the leading and the thousands of pieces of glass and understand better their design construction.

In England this was the period when Canterbury, York, Lancaster, Dorchester, and Abby were built. In France, Le Mans, Poitiers, St. Denis, Lyon, Strasbourg, and many others came into existence. In Germany, cathedrals built included Augsburg and Helmstedt. Characteristic of the era, the Bishop of St. Denis had virtually unlimited funds for construction of his cathedral.

The cathedrals of this era were designed by master builders and, with the aid of a faithful nobility and religious populace, took over a century to complete. The involvement of church, nobility, and commoner created a unity of performance and achievement in architecture and the arts that is rarely seen in history.

Well into the thirteenth century work continued on many structures begun the century before. Le Mans and Strasbourg were still being built, and new cathedrals were being started: The great Cathedral of Soissons and its beautiful stylized sculpture, Rheims, Rouen and its superb Rose Window, St. Chapelle with its glass jewel windows that are admired as a masterpiece by laymen and every glassmaker who has ever seen them.

The Cathedral of Chartres, one of the greatest of them all, was begun in the twelfth century, completed in the next. The windows of Chartres represent a triumph for all time in the art of stained glassmaking, an ultimate experience in the fusion of the art with spiritual philosophy and architectural form.

The windows served both to tell the stories of the Bible to an untutored population and to define the totality of the structure. The windows softened and diffused light within the Cathedral and retained the architectural scale of the interior, relieving the sharpness and hard edge of the structure. In effect, the transmission of light served to emphasize the Divinity by creating a special, mystical atmosphere, unmatched elsewhere in the church-goer's experience. The exalted size and design elevated the House of the Lord and thereby reduced the scale of man in his relation to his God.

The Late Gothic era of the fourteenth and early fifteenth centuries brought to a close this unparalleled period in the history of Christian art, an era that throughout its duration was one of intense religiosity, firm command by the Church, and a keen and immediate sense of personal involvement in the observance of the arts as part of the religious experience.

The stained-glass windows of this Medieval period define the art form at its best. It is here that the full impact of the medium can be observed. From the exterior of the Gothic church the windows are dark. Time and weathering have melded them into the structure. Upon entering the nave, the full brilliance and beauty impact upon the viewer, enveloping him in glowing splendor that has been enhanced by each scratch and blister of time which intensifies the brilliance like faceted gems.

In these structures the medium is used to its optimum potential. The windows are not paintings, nor are they merely illustrations depicting history. It is here that the simplicity of design, the integral leading, and the transformed color of the exterior light bring alive the skillful artistry and power of the window to create an environment that exhilarates the spirit and inspires full devotion and belief of man. This period was the high point of the living church, soon to be followed by an era of the liberated man.

Except for parts of Germany where the style was extended for a longer period of time, the Gothic design approach was constant throughout Europe well into the fourteenth century. While still under the Gothic dominance, new stirrings anticipated the turn to Humanism, not by a change of control or subject matter, but by a change in design.

In Austria windows were being produced by the Church in higher and more brilliant color and naïve simplicity of pattern, balanced by intricate and detailed paintings on the glass and bordered by highly stylized rich ornament. In the Cathedral of Cologne new windows also reflected a change. As in Austria, the color was more brilliant than before. Instead of being drawn flat, the figures have form and rhythmic curves. The draperies are free flowing. In the Chapel of Ehreichsdorf the design is also more sophisticated, with more modeling of heads and figures. Drapery is free flowing and less structured, and the window design seems more suitable to a court than to a chapel.

A change is becoming evident. Formalism has been encroached upon by Humanism. Even the Patron Bishop of Ratisbon found no problem in hanging his portrait, commissioned in stained glass. And backgrounds and borders appear in windows, designs of fabrics from the East, medallions and decorative foliage patterns that are less abstract and closer to Realism.

The trade of the earlier eras expanded and brought affluence to merchant families. In Italy the Sforzas, Gonzagas, Medici, Malatestas were building their dynasties. More and more large, secular structures were appearing on the scene. The nobility was consolidating its power, and the new merchant class was beginning to wield influence. The Church became more dependent upon these rising groups for funds, and battles and accommodation between the vying groups became a fact of society.

Simultaneous with these political and economic changes came a rebirth of interest in Classicism. Roman and Greek sculpture and art became of interest, as did ancient literature and science. Manuscripts that had lain in monasteries for centuries were sought out and read. Man's religious philosophy underwent a change from the belief that the human and natural world existed solely as the creation of God, to a new view of nature and all phenomena that could be looked upon not as a divine gift, but as an area for inquiry and investigation, in short, a science. The new merchants were securing their position, they sought titles and positions of power in the Church, even dreaming of taking over the control of the Church, an ambition shared equally by the nobility.

The merchants commissioned writers, artists, musicians, sculptors, and stained-glass design craftsmen to supply them with the environments and culture of the time. They called upon the same artists and craftsmen practitioners, but their needs were new. They did not require an art to teach the faith to an illiterate populace. Theirs was a need for prestige and the consolidation of power, and both of these needs could be in part fulfilled by surrounding themselves with the material display of cultural accomplishment that would underline their role as the new sponsors of the arts and leaders in society.

For the stained-glass designer, this necessitated a drastic change of direction. He was required to turn from solely religious patronage to a more intimate, lay-oriented patron. The stained-glass designer was expected to create genre scenes for installation in nonreligious structures. He was commissioned to design stained-glass windows honoring tournaments, successful courting experiences, hunting scenes, shields, emblems, and armorial glass panels. And if the patron desired a religious subject, the selection of theme was not made by the Church but by the merchant or nobleman who paid the money.

This new orientation and new market brought another significant change. The closed shop or guild, which had previously controlled the design and making of stained glass, lost its monopoly. The artists were no longer confined under the guild system to work in only one craft. They could design in many media. The field was open. An artist now could execute commissions in painting, sculpture, stained glass, prints, tapestry, and even architecture. This was the era of the new freedom.

From this new activity that was transforming Europe, the stained-glass designer obtained a new patron and client. The building of secular structures increased. The same men who dreamed and schemed to name the future Cardinals and Popes for Christendom related pragmatically to the culture of the known world.

This new era of the individual emerging toward the end of the fifteenth century introduced the era of the Renaissance, a period of private patronage and political popes. Artists and craftsmen became more free to express their creative talents in a less structured manner. Religious subjects were still executed in stained glass, but the work represented the special style of the individual artist-craftsman and not the overriding style of period and structure as in the centuries before.

In his design of a window depicting the coronation of the Virgin, Donatello created a realistic interpretation that, despite its beauty, could not likely have been conceived, much less accepted, in prior centuries. Ambrogio Lorenzetti's *St. Michael, the Archangel,* in Siena, is much too realistic and figurative to speak to a Gothic culture. His model could well have been the man next door. His work forecast the figurative and literal direction of design to come.

Lorenzo Ghiberti's *The Prayers in the Garden City of Jerusalem* no longer has the symmetry of design that characterized the windows of the past. It is a bold personal statement. The mind of Leonardo da Vinci was exploring beyond religious scripture. Michelangelo was writing love poetry, and Machiavelli was preparing an action manual to help a Medici consolidate his power. The new freedom was reflected in the works. It is a new era, one in which man is an ultimate entity, no longer subordinate to church and God as in the Medieval period when cathedrals were scaled to diminish the position of man. New types of stained-glass commissions were available, and there were men of many talents to execute them.

Stained-glass panels were made for many of the guilds by anyone from goldsmiths to butchers. The Medici coat of arms was designed and made in glass for the Biblioteca Laurenziano Florence. Mythical, grotesque scenes were made for the Palazzo Vecchio in Florence. A St. Michael window displaying the Fleur-de-lis was purchased by a Royal patron. A St. George in Flemish family armor satisfied a client's contribution to his church. A warrior with a flag was a secular commission for Schaffhausen Church. Various commissions were available for stained glass-makers—requests for roundels, coats of arms, designs for town halls and guild halls. Swiss heraldic windows in sizable quantities established a standard of six to nine pieces of glass. Genre scenes in glass, made in Holland by Jacob Cornelisz, were in demand.

The new market required a more figurative approach. There was more modeling of the figures and draperies, less pure stylized design, more deep tones and colors. While the market for stained glass increased, the number of artists seeking commissions exceeded the demand. Many painters looked for and accepted commissions. Nicolo da Varallo executed a series of stained-glass windows for the Cathedral of Milan on the subject of making the royal throne. Paolo Vecello, a most able painter with a superb sense of design, created a series of windows for the Santa Maria in Florence. Domenico Ghirlandaio, who painted panels in the Sistine Chapel, designed border patterns for a client. Dirt Vellert, a printmaker, executed a stained-glass commission for King's College in Cambridge on a series of windows titled *Life of Christ.*

By the end of the Renaissance all remnants of the Gothic and its simplicity, power, and direct use of medium as dominant design element were gone. We enter the seventeenth century with many people designing windows but a declining number understanding the medium.

In Switzerland and Holland stained glass was being produced for screens in homes, personal rooms, and other lay purposes. Companies were being organized to meet the new art demands of the affluent merchants. These new enterprises were no longer the anonymous stained-glass guilds of the Gothic nor even the individualized expressions and interpretations from the artist workshops of the Renaissance, but rather an entirely new kind of business-oriented workshop with new techniques and practices.

The work in stained glass sharply declined in quality. The spirit of most of the glass artisans diminished, and while many designed windows, only a few remotely understood the power of the medium and its potential. Design was affected by the practice of painting on glass with enamels and firing the glass to a semi-obscure surface, a process that resulted in no brilliance and greatly reduced transmittal of light.

There was little attempt to relate a stained-glass window to architecture. Stained-glass portraits were made, such as for Charles I, that were pure painting, albeit on glass, that had no relation to the medium but were simply blown up pictures of miniatures. The decline continued through the next two centuries, undergoing transformation from personalized craft to a factory operation that turned out made-to-order products. Design became weaker. Stock sections for borders were made in advance and related poorly to the final work.

In almost every respect, the eighteenth century was a disaster for the art of stained glass. The church work was predominantly figurative painting on glass that further screened out light from the undistinguished structure in which they were installed. Even reputable artists like Sir Joshua Reynolds tried their hand at the craft and produced poor paintings on glass that showed no comprehension of the power of the medium when correctly used.

Indeed, the understanding of stained glass as a unique and spectacular art form seems to have been lost. Example after example produced during this era of splendid courts and prospering commerce shows no grasp of the understanding that the medium owes its artistic existence to light. Instead of employing the colored glass and leading as direct design elements, glassmakers worked on the glass itself in a manner that diminished its brilliance and distorted the medium.

Partly to blame was the elaborate and ornate style that came so much into vogue, Rococo, the antithesis of the Gothic which directly equated the design of an object to its material. Rococo, on the contrary, designed for the sake of embellishment, and its success in covering every surface with intricate detail largely eliminated the need for stained glass as adornment.

Nor was the intellectual and spiritual climate receptive to creation of meaningful works of art. The Age of Enlightenment had further loosened the hold of the Church on men's minds, the rising firmament of revolution and hostility of the common man to both Church and nobility had quite destroyed the base for broad patronage of the arts.

Another cause for the decline of stained glassmakers and, indeed, all of the artisan crafts was the rise of mechanization that began first in England and soon spread throughout the western world. This phenomenon, which for lack of a better term we call the Industrial Revolution, reoriented all concepts of society and came close to destroying handcrafts of all types.

There were men like William Morris who were sensitive to the decline in the arts and who greatly admired the Medieval period and encouraged creative craft. Morris sponsored Burne-Jones to design a window on the theme of St. Frideswide and Rosetta to create one on St. George and the Dragon in the effort to revitalize stained glassmaking as a creative activity. John Ruskin, the English writer and critic in the arts, also called for reestablishment of values in this discipline. Their voices were to little avail. The dislocations brought to the whole realm of handcraft and the arts by an emergent industrialism were overwhelming and beyond the powers of mere individuals to influence.

Not really until midway through the twentieth century did stained glass come to life again as a vital craft medium, once again expressing the spirit of an era. Following the end of the second world war, a new religious stirring was felt, not in the mold of previous eras but rather as a commitment of small congregations, desirous of creating new and contemporary structures to complete the new suburban communities that were building up. Many new religious institutions were built, and the need was felt by the congregations, their religious leaders, and the architects who designed the new churches and temples to make provision for various kinds of art work and for the installation of stained-glass windows. Indeed, the commissioning of ceremonial sculpture, tapisrugs, and stained glass constitutes a twentieth century Renaissance in works commissioned, not only by religious institutions, but by lay institutions as well.

To meet this need, many stained-glass fabricating companies came into existence to design and produce the work. Some of the windows produced in these shops are of excellent quality. Unfortunately, many of the creative artists associated with these shops are not known. Unlike the ateliers of Rubens or Finlandia which featured the artist, the contemporary name is more likely to be that of the businessman in whose name the work is commissioned, or the shop crafting it.

Still, there are many artists and designers whose work in stained glass is of superb quality that ranks in conception and understanding of the medium with great works of the past. Others, for lack of understanding of the medium, are making paintings that are then translated into glass by workshops which, although they may be excellent in their craft, are not able to disguise the fact that a painting translated into glass does not fulfill the potential of a stained-glass window.

Examples of successful stained-glass designs by an artist are the windows designed by Henri Matisse for the Chapel at Vence in southern France. The beauty of these simple windows stems from the artist's understanding of the function of light within space. The freshness of the design and the cheerfulness of the environment speak well for this artist's genius. The windows were executed by Paul Bony who successfully retained all aspects of Matisse's design.

Another world renowned painter, Marc Chagall, has created many stained-glass windows—one at Tudely Kent in England; a series for Hadassah Hospital in Ein Karim, Israel; and others in Germany and the United States. They are interesting paintings translated into glass, a perfect example of the misuse of the stained-glass potential. They are interesting paintings but poor stained-glass windows.

Fernand Léger's three panels for the Church at Audincourt, executed by others, are a direct abstract use of stained-glass techniques in a contemporary idiom. His floor to ceiling windows in the Baptistry are a contemporary masterpiece.

Georges Rouault, the great French painter whose paintings frequently look like drawings in stained glass, designed six windows at Assy. It is unfortunate that Rouault did not receive more stained-glass commissions in his lifetime. Those that he did create are masterful. Paul Bony, who executed the windows for Matisse in Vence, also produced the windows for Rouault.

There are many other stained-glass artists, designers, and craftsmen who are creating significant works of art in stained glass. Heinz Bienefeld's wall in the Church of St. Mary the Queen, near Cologne, is a contemporary architectural solution of outstanding beauty. Alfred Manessier's Chapel at Hem, France, of abstract bold shapes and strong color is in the best of design concepts, as is Ben Shahn's linear design for a Temple in Buffalo, New York, and the series of small windows at Varangeville by Georges Braque.

Other artists having the opportunity to design in the medium include John Piper, Geoffrey Clark, and others in England who received stained-glass commissions as part of the rebuilding of Coventry and Liverpool Cathedrals.

Although stained glass has been primarily commissioned for churches, there are many commissions available for homes, pub-

lic buildings, business, industry, and institutions. Fairview Park Hospital in Ohio commissioned LeRoy Flint to create a small window in a reception area. K.L.M. Airlines commissioned Gyorgy Kepes to design a window in the company's New York City Office. Theatrical Restaurant commissioned a window for its cocktail lounge.

Since Tiffany created hanging light shades and other stained-glass objects for homes, there has been an increasing interest in the use of this unique medium which enhanced environment by harnessing the power of light through colored glass. While much of the work created is of little esthetic consequence, the medium lends itself to creative opportunities and new applications. We are today very much in an era of exploration of new solutions to old problems in all areas of our experience. This era, much like times past, will find the solutions that best represent the culture and society of our time.

Leon Gordon Miller

STAINED-
GLASS
CRAFT

INTRODUCTION

The processes of stained-glass crafting continue to remain an enigma despite the recent upsurge of interest in the craft. To the casual observer, the techniques involved appear to be far beyond the ability of the novice to acquire. The high price tags usually attached to stained-glass items further reinforce the idea that stained glass must be the product of highly guarded craft skills passed down from generation to generation.

To the contrary, almost any commercially made stained-glass object can be produced in the home workshop using ordinary household tools at a small fraction of its retail cost. Though the craft has undergone many changes since its beginning, the basic techniques remain largely unchanged. Fortunately, however, many improvements have been made in both the quality and variety of glass and equipment used. As will become quickly apparent, no special equipment not already part of most home workshops is required to carry out the projects described in this text.

This text does not purport to offer a complete course in the techniques of stained glass, nor does it attempt to cover every aspect of the craft. Instead, this book treats the basic processes involved in constructing modern stained-glass lamps, windows, and other projects. The step-by-step instructional approach treats each phase in proper sequence from the acquisition of all needed materials to the assembly of the final product. But more important than the final product is the ability to transfer knowledge and skills to other projects of your own creation.

Every effort has been made to simplify the procedures and technical aspects of the craft. Whenever traditional techniques and equipment can be replaced by simpler and more modern methods, the latter have been recommended. The text presumes no knowledge of either glass cutting or soldering techniques on the part of the reader. Consequently, portions of the text are devoted to explaining the required basics as they are needed in the sequence of steps to complete a particular project.

The author wishes to express his sincere appreciation to the many people whose contributions made possible the creation of this book. In particular the author wishes to thank Leon Gordon Miller; John F. Eilers, Jr.; Kenneth L. Kimmins; and Kenny Darst for sharing their knowledge and skills accumulated over many years of professional practice in the field of stained glass. In addition, two very talented men, Peter Fromm and Philip F. Vaughn, deserve recognition for their respective contributions in the areas of photography and art illustration.

1

WHAT YOU'LL NEED TO BEGIN

Stained Glass

Art glass is not just stained. Instead, art glass or "stained glass" is colored throughout in the molten state by the addition of metals and oxides to the basic glass ingredients. In its various forms, copper produces green, blue, or an intense red. Purple, violet, brown, and even black are made by adding manganese. We are fortunate that modern technology has made an almost infinite variety of colors available.

Stained glass may be classified into several basic types:

Rolled glass   This is the most common variety of stained glass. Rolled into flat sheets of regular texture and thickness, it is furnished in smooth or hammered finishes produced by rolling in patterns when the glass is in the plastic state. This type of glass is highly recommended for the beginner because of its relatively low cost and even ⅛-inch thickness.

Antique glass This is a form of glass made by the antique method of hand blowing molten glass into a cylindrical form, removing the top and bottom of the cylinder, cutting the glass cylinder lengthwise, and firing it to the point where the cylinder is opened and flattened onto the kiln shelf. As a handmade glass, its cost is normally several times that of rolled glass; thickness variations, although contributing to the inherent beauty of the glass, make working with antique glass more difficult. One variation of antique glass is "flashed glass"—a thin film or flash of color on a backing of white or clear glass. Using acid, the flash is etched away where desired, leaving only transparent or white areas where the acid has acted.

Dalle or slab glass This is used primarily for faceted or glass panels by embedding the dalles in a matrix of epoxy or concrete. Molten glass is simply ladled into an 8″ x 12″ x 1″ open mold. Dalles vary in thickness from 7/8 to about one inch. Faceting is usually done to one face to produce a jewellike effect.

Roundels This is handspun ornamental glass which is "gathered" or collected in molten form and blown into a ball. The glowing glass is then spun out to its desired size and separated from the pipe. The familiar irregular center, known as a "pontil" mark, is where separation has taken place.

Norman slabs This is a rather uncommon rectangular glass that is thick at the center and thin at the edges. Norman slabs are produced by blowing molten glass into a four-sided mold, removing the top and bottom, and slicing the mold at the corners.

It was previously suggested that the beginner use glass of even thickness to eliminate problems in applying lead cames. For this reason, rolled glass is highly recommended.

Before beginning the actual construction of a lamp or window, you will find it worthwhile to purchase some irregularly shaped pieces of glass (scrap glass) for practice in using the glass cutter

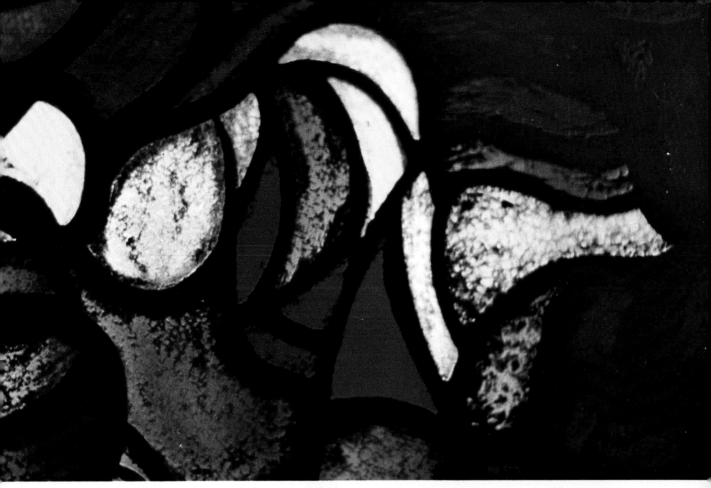

Window.

LEON GORDON MILLER

The Three Kings.

BRONE JAMEIKIS

Sails.

Mosaic coffee table.

effectively. Manufacturers of stained glass as well as stained-glass studios usually have scrap glass piles where small but useful glass remnants can be selected at low cost. Glass is usually sold by the square foot at stained-glass studios and, of course, its cost varies from studio to studio. Most studios will slice off a piece from a stock sheet (32″ x 60-84″) according to your requirements. When you begin making projects, use good quality rather than attempting to accumulate enough scrap glass of the same color and texture. This will mean paying a little more, but the enjoyment you receive from the finished project will more than offset the price difference.

Lead Cames

Lead cames, or channeled lead, are available in a variety of sizes and types. Fortunately, you need purchase only one size which will suffice for a number of projects.

A good size came to begin with is the ¼-inch round (Fig. 1-1), a common lead came used in church windows and readily available through most stained-glass studios. Should ¼-inch cames not be available, a larger size is preferable to a smaller one.

Fig. 1-1. Common lead sizes.

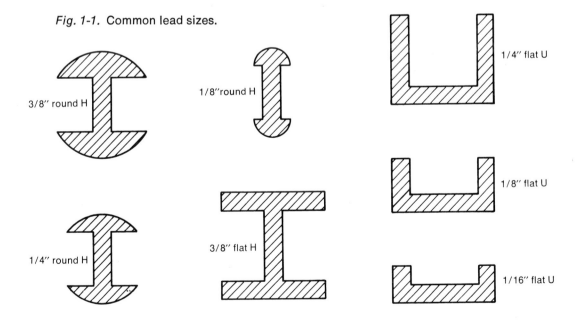

3/8″ round H

1/8″round H

1/4″ flat U

1/4″ round H

3/8″ flat H

1/8″ flat U

1/16″ flat U

Lead cames are commonly sold in lengths of six feet before stretching, with each length weighing approximately one pound, depending on size. Although you will need only about eight lengths for the Tiffany-style lamp, you might want to inquire about buying a greater quantity and receiving a discount, particularly if you are planning other stained-glass projects. The amount of lead required for a stained-glass window will, of course, vary with the size and detail involved in its construction.

The Work Area

The worktable consists of any flat wooden surface at least 2' x 5' in dimension. Although any wooden surface can be used, plywood seems to withstand rough treatment better than other materials. Adequate overhead lighting is also important if eye strain is to be avoided.

Straight wooden strips (about 1" x 2") nailed securely along the left and bottom edges of the table provide a supportive straight edge against which most of the work will be placed during construction.

The only other tools needed are a bench vise for straightening lead cames and a wooden mitre box for cutting multiple pieces of

Fig. 1-2. Worktable with mitre box and vise.

lead to the same length (Fig. 1-2). Any size vise will do but a bolt-down type secured to one corner of the worktable is preferable to the clamp-on vise. The mitre box, constructed of rock maple, may be securely fastened to the same side of the worktable opposite the vise. Only one modification of the mitre box is needed. A strip of wood (a leftover piece of the table edge strip) should be nailed to the bottom of the mitre box to raise the cutting level. The strip should be high enough to enable the saw blade to cut into the surface of the wooden strip.

Soldering Equipment

To begin, you will need the proper type of electric soldering iron. Probably the most common type is the "gun" design which produces heat quickly when the trigger is depressed but is not designed for continuous heat output. Since stained-glass crafting requires extensive soldering, an iron designed for continuous operation is recommended. A broad tip about ½-inch wide should also be used since most soldering is done using the flat surface of the soldering tip. The Sears 200-watt heavy duty electric iron pictured in Fig. 1-3 is highly recommended for stained-glass crafting.

The right kind of wire solder is essential if soldered joints are

Fig. 1-3. Soldering equipment.

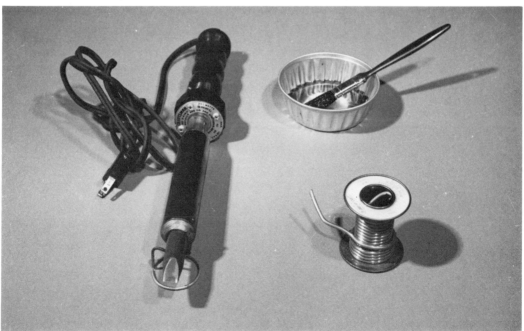

Fig. 1-4. Additional tools.

Additional Craft Materials for Leader Glass (Fig. 1-4)

1. Glass cutter (steel wheel)
2. Two dozen 1- or 1½-inch nails or brads
3. Claw hammer
4. Hacksaw
5. "T" square
6. Three metal-edge wooden rulers
7. Pliers
8. Lead pencil with blunted point
9. Container of light oil
10. Trowel (about 2-inch blade)
11. Retractable knife

to be made correctly. Solder is composed of various combinations of tin and lead. Because tin melts at a lower temperature than lead, solder of a high tin content is desirable. Ordinary solder containing 50 percent tin and 50 percent lead (50/50) is not recommended. A solid wire solder containing 60 percent tin and 40 percent lead (60/40) will melt at a lower temperature, flow on the soldered surface more evenly, and reduce the chance of burning the lead cames. A one-pound spool of solder is sufficient for a number of projects.

Soldering flux is just as important as the proper iron and solder. Oleic acid, a common laboratory chemical, is used widely as a flux in stained-glass work. Oleic acid may be purchased readily at most pharmacies or chemical supply houses. Several ounces and a small brush are all you need.

2

THE MODERN TIFFANY

Glass Cutting

USING THE GLASS CUTTER EFFECTIVELY

Cutting glass requires no special skill or equipment other than a steel wheel glass cutter. The cutter is held perpendicular to the worktable between the thumb and index finger with the thumb supporting the cutter on the underside (Fig. 2-1). A single score or mark is made on the glass surface beginning at the top edge and drawing the cutter over the surface and toward the body, allowing the cutter to run off the bottom edge of the glass onto the wooden surface. It is important that only a single score be made on the glass since retracing the score line will often result in splintering.

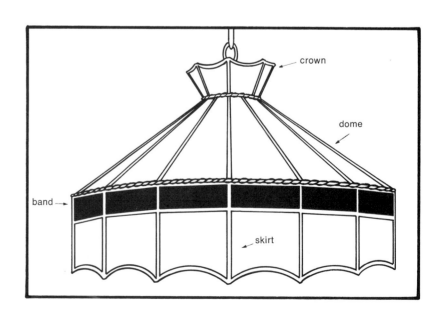

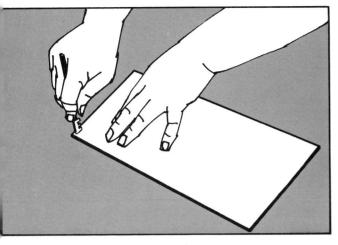

Fig. 2-1. Position for cutting glass.

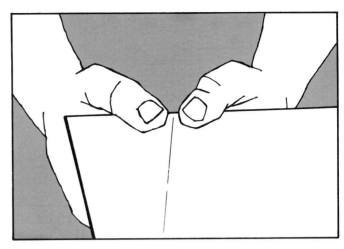

Fig. 2-2. Breaking at the score line.

Fig. 2-3. Removing small piece with pliers.

Fig. 2-4. Scraping to remove sharp edges.

When the score is made, the glass should be held with the score line between the two thumbs near the bottom edge of the glass. A slight downward pressure will cause separation at the score line (Fig. 2-2).

If a narrow piece of glass is to be cut from a larger piece, enough leverage probably cannot be obtained using the thumbs. In this case, hold the piece of glass with the left hand as described above and the right side with a plier at the score line. The same downward pressure will cause the glass to separate (Fig. 2-3).

To avoid the possibility of cut fingers, the edges of both separated pieces should be gently scraped against each other to remove sharp edges (Fig. 2-4).

Practice using the glass cutter before proceeding to cut the component parts. Using scrap glass, draw the cutter freehand across the surface of the glass and then use a straight edge as a guide. When you begin to feel comfortable using the glass cutter, you are ready to cut the component glass parts.

CUTTING THE DOME COMPONENT

Making the diagonal and straight cuts for a Tiffany-style lamp can be easily accomplished using three metal-edge wooden rules (12-inch size) commonly required for school use. Two rulers are nailed to the worktable parallel to one another, with the third rule (metal edge to the right) nailed perpendicular to the bottom ruler (Fig. 2-5). This simple ruler jig is all that is needed for cutting all glass component parts.

To begin, 16 pieces of glass will be needed to form the dome of the lamp. A piece of glass 8 inches wide by about 52 inches long will provide more than enough glass for this component part.

Start by carefully tracing the piece of glass (Fig. 2-6) onto a piece of heavy paper and carefully cut out along the traced line. Place the paper pattern on the jig and align the metal edge of the ruler to match the angle of the paper pattern (Fig. 2-7). After the angle has been set, secure the upper end of the ruler with a nail to prevent movement.

Remove the paper pattern and insert the 8-inch strip of glass under the cutting bar (angled ruler) and snug against the bottom ruler guide. Using the glass cutter and the cutting bar as a guide, cut and remove a small portion of the glass (Fig. 2-8).

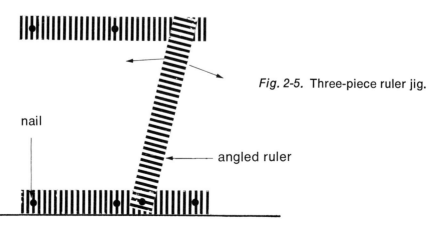

nail

Fig. 2-5. Three-piece ruler jig.

angled ruler

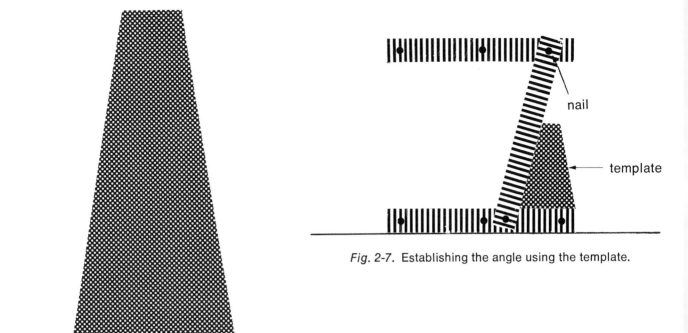

Fig. 2-7. Establishing the angle using the template.

nail

template

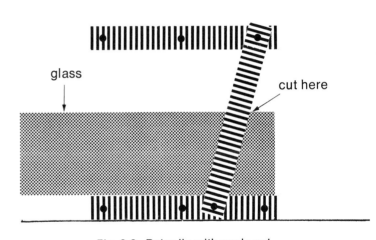

glass

cut here

Fig. 2-8. Ruler jig with angle set.

A B

Fig. 2-6. Template for dome component.

31

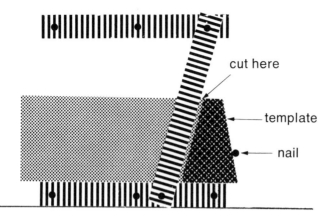

Fig. 2-9. Using template to set lateral dimension.

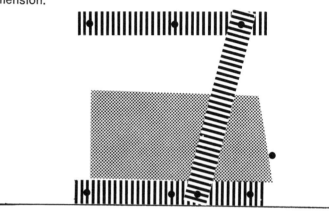

Fig. 2-10. Ruler jig set for repetitive cutting.

Remove and reverse the glass strip. Insert it again under the cutting bar so that the diagonal cut remains on the same end, but the opposite face of the glass is now visible.

Replace the paper pattern over the glass and align the bottom and right edges. When holding the pattern and the glass together, position the glass so that the glass cutter, held against the cutting bar, will exactly hit the edge of the paper pattern. When this adjustment has been made, place a nail anywhere along the right side of the glass as a stop (Fig. 2-9).

You are now ready to cut the first of 16 pieces of glass. Score along the cutting bar and remove the piece of glass as previously described (Fig. 2-10). This separated piece of glass should match the paper pattern exactly.

Remove the glass strip; reverse it again using the same end but opposite face. Reinsert under the cutting bar to the nail stop. Make the score and separate as before (Fig. 2-10). It should be evident that each piece is cut using the iterative process of reversing, reinserting, and cutting the strip of glass until all 16 pieces of glass have been cut.

This basic process will be used for each of the three remaining components of the Tiffany-style lamp as well as other types of suspended fixtures. As you will see, the cutting of each component glass piece requires a simple variation of the ruler angle to reset the jig.

CUTTING THE BAND

The band (Fig. 2-11) is the easiest component to cut since it involves neither angular cuts nor continual reversing of the glass in the jig. Like the dome, the band is composed of 16 pieces which may be cut from a strip of glass about 1 inch wide by about 52 inches long. Although the width may vary according to personal preference, dimension AB of the band must match exactly AB of the dome (Fig. 2-12). If the dome pieces do not match exactly the template in Fig. 2-6, use the actual AB dimension of the dome component you have already cut to determine the critical length of the band.

A   B

Fig. 2-11. Template for band.

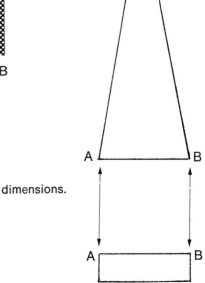

Fig. 2-12. Matching dome and band dimensions.

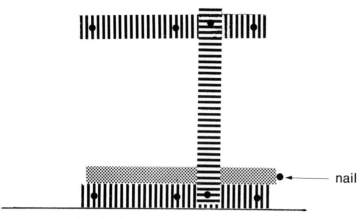

Fig. 2-13. Ruler jig set for cutting band.

nail

A simple modification of the ruler jig is needed to cut all the band pieces to proper length. Since the band is a rectangle, the jig should be set up as shown in Fig. 2-13. Note that the nail stop is placed so the 1-inch wide strip inserted against the stop will exactly match the dome component. As you did in cutting the dome, be sure to allow for the cutter wheel and to test for proper matching after the first piece is cut. If adjustments are needed, simply move the nail stop slightly to the left or right. The remaining pieces are cut, of course, by feeding the band strip through the jig after each cut.

CUTTING THE SKIRT

The skirt (Fig. 2-14), like the band, is also a rectangle with a curvilinear cut made after all pieces have been cut into their rectangular shape. Composed of 16 pieces, the skirt requires a strip of glass about 52 inches in length with a width of about 4 inches. No jig adjustments will be needed for the skirt since the jig has already been set for rectangular cutting and dimension AB of the skirt will perfectly match those of the band and dome. Follow the same procedure as you did for the band. When all 16 pieces have been cut, you are ready to make the curvilinear cut that will result in the scalloped edge along the bottom.

Using heavy paper, cut out a pattern to match the skirt piece. Before making the actual cut, practice on scrap glass until you are able to make the score smoothly and accurately. It is impor-

A   B

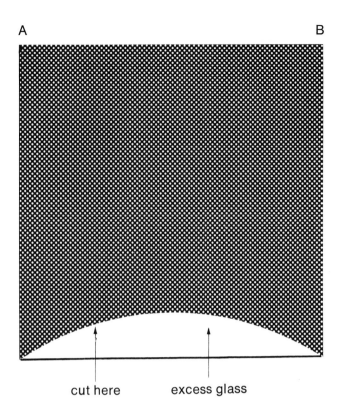

cut here   excess glass

Fig. 2-14. Template for skirt.

tant that the score be made as a smooth unbroken line since an irregular cut will cause a break to occur at the point where the score is interrupted. Place the pattern over the rectangular skirt piece and score along the curved line. Lightly tapping the underside of the glass along the score line will allow the excess to break away easily (Fig. 2-15).

Fig. 2-15. Tapping curvilinear cut from underside.

CUTTING THE CROWN

The last of the glass components (Fig. 2-16) consists of only eight pieces cut from a strip of glass 2 inches wide by about 21 inches long. This length allows for several additional pieces since the probability of breakage is increased during the assembly of the crown. If the dome component has been cut according to pattern, two pieces of glass cut for the dome with a 1/16-inch separation for the lead came should equal exactly the small end of the crown (Fig. 2-17). If the dome pieces were not made precisely to pattern, be sure to adjust the crown dimension to those of the two dome pieces. Assuming no adjustments are necessary, trace Fig. 2-16 onto heavy paper and place in the jig. The techniques of setting the angle for the crown are just as described for the dome in Figures 2-7 through 2-10. When 10 or 11 pieces have been cut (to allow for breakage), place the paper pattern over each piece and make the curvilinear cut for the crown in the same way that you did for the skirt.

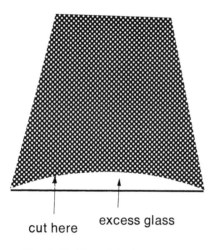

cut here   excess glass

Fig. 2-16. Template for crown.

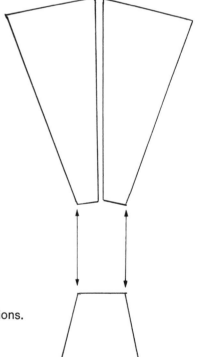

Fig. 2-17. Matching dome and crown dimensions.

Lead Cutting

Channeled lead must be straightened before cutting and fitting for component construction. Straightening is accomplished by using an ordinary bench vise attached to one end of the work-table. One end of the lead strip is securely clamped in the vise and the other held with the pliers. Twists and kinks may be removed by twisting the strip in the opposite direction and simultaneously stretching the lead several inches or until perfectly straight (Fig. 2-18).

Fig. 2-18. Stretching lead to remove kinks.

SETTING UP A MITRE BOX

A hardwood mitre box with a wooden strip nailed securely to its base serves as a valuable tool that will take the guesswork out of cutting multiple lead strips to uniform lengths (Fig. 2-19). Stained-glass studios generally use a modified version of a table saw to accomplish the same purpose. Using a simple mitre box, though a little more time consuming, will produce equally good results.

Fig. 2-19. Mitre box for cutting lead cames.

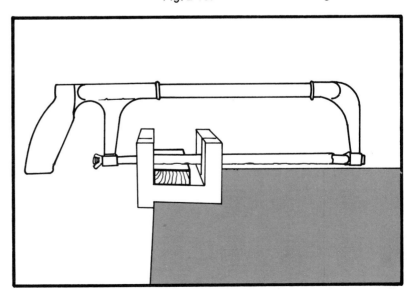

Lead cames must be cut precisely so there will be no gaps between joining lead cames. If each lead strip is cut about ⅛ inch shorter (1/16 inch on each end) than the glass that it supports, top and bottom leads will fit properly with no gaps between leads (Fig. 2-20).

Fig. 2-20. Lead cut to proper size.

CUTTING LEADS TO FIT COMPONENTS

Prior to constructing the component parts, lead strips will be needed in the designated quantities for each of the glass pieces as shown in Fig. 2-21. The first lead came of each size should be cut with a hand knife, using the glass piece as a guide.

To set the mitre box for the first cut, place the hacksaw between the 90-degree slots on the right side and the hand cut lead strip snugly against the left side of the blade. Then place a small nail against the left end of the lead to serve as a stop (Fig. 2-22). Subsequent leads of the same size are fed into the jig to the stop and cut by drawing the hacksaw blade toward the bottom edge of the worktable (Fig. 2-23). A sharp blade is essential to avoid crushing the lead through excess cutting pressure.

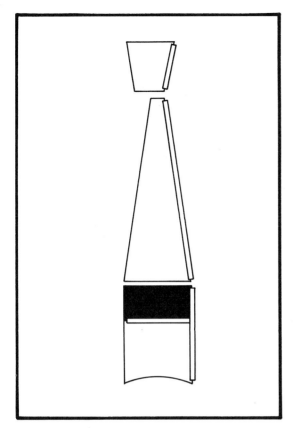

Fig. 2-21. Lead cames needed.

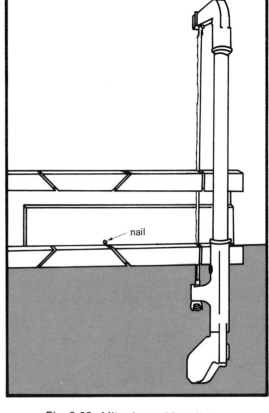

Fig. 2-22. Mitre box with nail stop.

Fig. 2-23. Mitre box with lead in position for cutting.

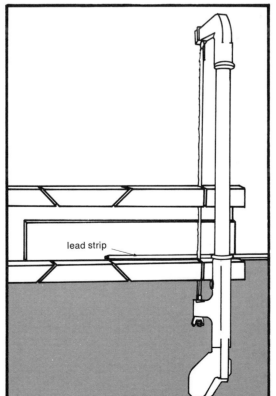

39

ASSEMBLY OF ALTERNATE GLASS AND LEAD PIECES

You may begin with any of the three major components—the crown, dome, or skirt-band. If you begin with the assembly of the dome, nail a small wood block near the bottom left side of the worktable and place the first glass piece, shiny side up, against the wood block (Fig. 2-24). The outer perimeter lead circle is formed by using a long lead strip which will be cut to proper size after all glass and lead pieces are in place. Be certain that the large end of each glass piece fits snugly into the channel of the perimeter lead. Run the blunt end of a lead pencil through the channel if the glass does not readily fit. As each glass piece is placed into position, gently tap the right edge with a block of wood to insure that each piece fits snugly into its adjoining lead (Fig. 2-25). Place nails on the small end of the glass pieces and the outer edge of the perimeter lead to prevent

Fig. 2-24. First dome piece in position for assembly.

Fig. 2-25. Assembling alternate glass and lead pieces.

movement. Next, place one matched strip of lead between the first and second glass pieces. Continue the repetitive process until all 16 pieces form an open circle (Fig. 2-26). The inner circle is made of lead and is formed last. Simply move all nails securing the small ends of the glass. Cut a strip of lead about 12 inches in length and form into a smaller circle than is actually needed (Fig. 2-27). Fit all the small ends into the lead channel expanding the circle as each end is gently pushed into the lead (Fig. 2-28). Replace several nails on the outer edge of the inner circle to hold it in place while soldering.

The crown is assembled in much the same manner; however, only eight pieces are used instead of 16. Using the same block of wood, alternate the placement of glass and lead until an open circle is formed (Fig. 2-29). The scalloped outer edge will require slightly more care in applying the outer perimeter lead circle. Complete the inner circle following the same procedure outlined for the dome component.

Fig. 2-26. Dome pieces assembled to form open circle.

Fig. 2-27. Forming small lead inner circle.

Fig. 2-28. Positioning inner circle lead.

Fig. 2-29. Crown pieces assembled to form open circle.

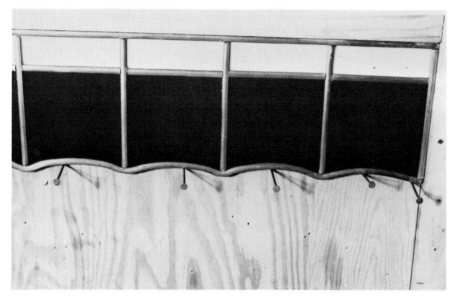

Fig. 2-30. Assembled skirt-band component.

The skirt component is actually composed of two separate glass pieces—the rectangular band and the scalloped skirt—together with their matching leads. Begin by nailing a wooden block at the left end of the worktable perpendicular to the wooden strip along the bottom edge. Place a length of lead (about 5 feet) against the bottom wood edge. Assemble band and skirt pieces as shown in Fig. 2-30. Be sure to gently tap the right edge of the glass pieces with a block of wood as you did when assembling the dome. When all 32 pieces are in place, remove nails from the outer edge and carefully fit a strip of lead onto the scalloped edge. Replace nails as needed on the outer edge of the perimeter lead to hold securely during soldering.

APPLYING BASIC SOLDERING TECHNIQUES

The techniques of soldering are easy to master if the proper materials and tools are used and some simple steps are followed. Where leads intersect, the broad flat soldering surface of the iron should be used while the pointed tip is reserved for small spaces.

44

Effective soldering requires a properly "tinned" soldering tip. Tinning is accomplished by applying a small amount of solder together with zinc chloride flux to the hot soldering tip. Because the tinning agent and the flux recommended for lead soldering contain repelling substances, be sure to wipe off all traces of zinc chloride flux before proceeding to solder lead. The tinning procedure should be repeated whenever soldering becomes difficult.

Before soldering the component parts, it is advisable to practice on scrap lead to get the feel of the iron. You will quickly become adept at knowing how hot your iron must be to cause an even flow of solder over the joint without burning through the lead came (Fig. 2-31).

Brush a small amount of oleic acid flux (using a separate brush) onto scrap lead. If the lead has oxidized with age, it will be necessary to clean the area to be soldered lightly with steel wool. Hold a length of wire solder directly over the joint and bring the broad surface of the soldering tip into contact with the solder and the lead. The solder should flow smoothly over the area that has been coated with flux.

Fig. 2-31. Soldering the dome.

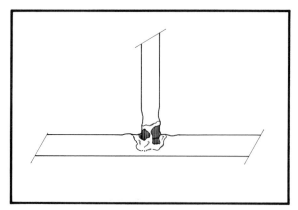

Fig. 2-32. Lead burned—iron too hot.

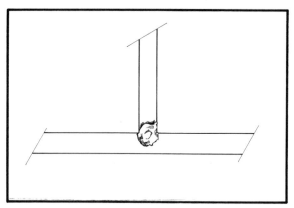

Fig. 2-33. Unmelted solder—iron not hot enough.

If the iron is too hot, or if excessive pressure is used, the lead came will be melted along with the solder (Fig. 2-32); if the iron is not hot enough, the solder will form an unmelted bead on the lead surface (Fig. 2-33). Testing the iron's temperature on scrap lead is highly recommended during the actual soldering of the components until you are able to judge temperature while soldering. To reduce the temperature of an iron, unplug it periodically and allow it to cool.

While the first face of each component piece is being soldered, nail supports should remain in place to prevent any movement of the work. When soldered, remove all nails, reverse the component, and solder all joints on the opposite face.

FORMING AND JOINING COMPONENT PARTS

Each of the three component parts must be formed or curved from its flat two-dimensional plane. For esthetic purposes, the shiny face should appear on the outside of the lamp on all three components. Depending on the color selection, several types of glass with various textured surfaces may be used in a single lamp. Using the shiny or smooth surfaces on the exterior will play down these differences.

When curving, breakage can be controlled by making certain that each lead cross strip is bent only a few degrees at a time (Fig. 2-34) until a circle is formed (Fig. 2-35). If breakage does

Transom.

R. KENNETH S. FOLTZ

K. L. KIMMINS

Faceted glass.

Faceted glass.

DR. KENNETH S. FOLTZ

Farbigem panel.

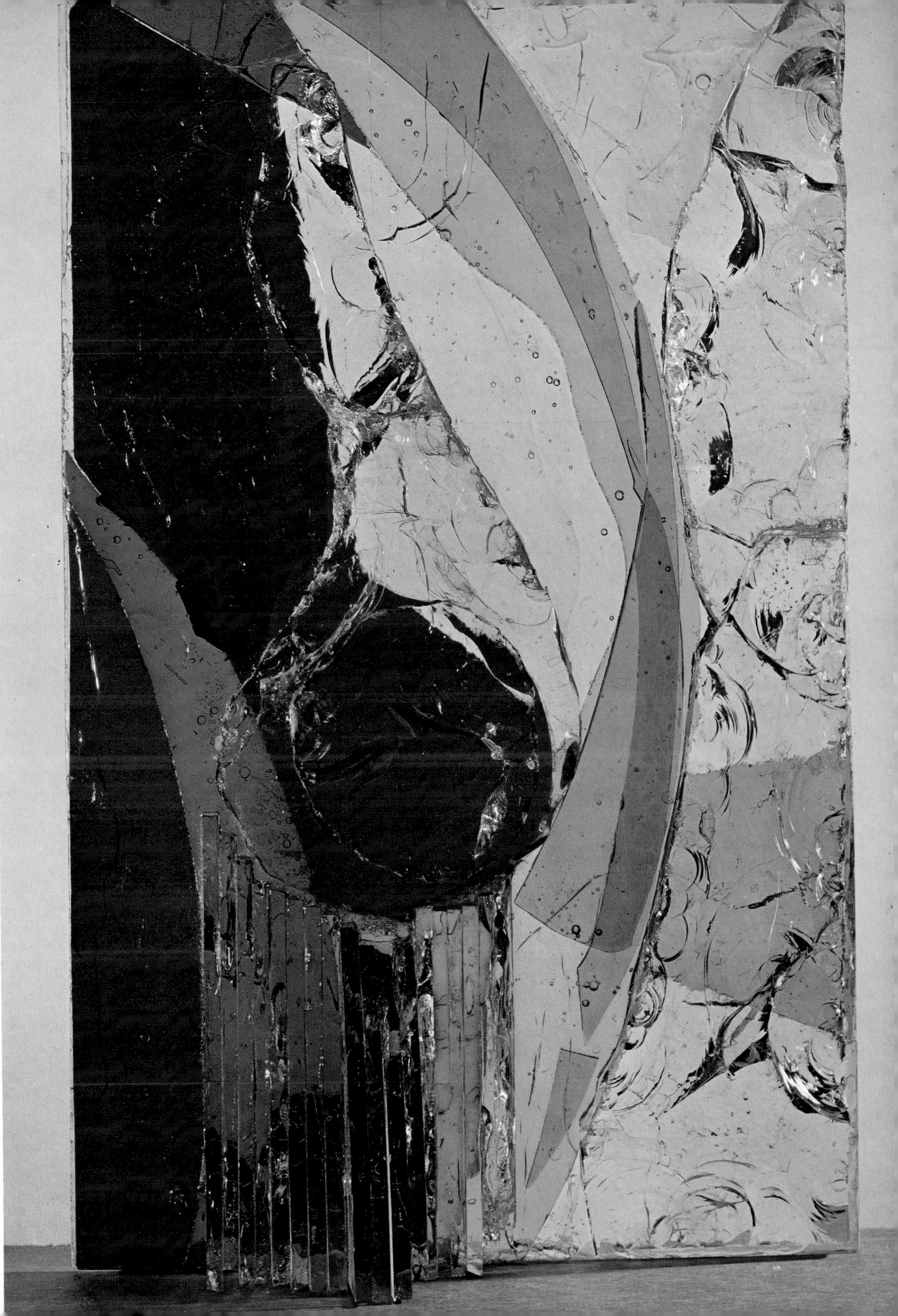

WORK OF WILLET STUDIOS

Faceted glass.

Avery's Window.

Fig. 2-34. Bending at cross leads.

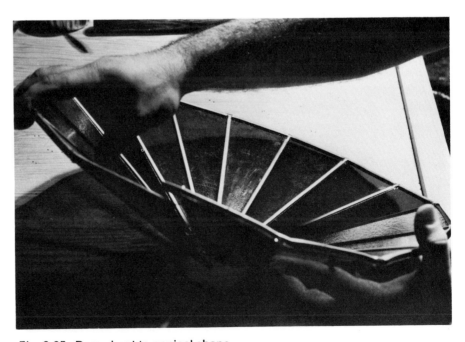

Fig. 2-35. Dome bent to conical shape.

47

occur while bending, continue curving and replace the broken piece after the component has been curved and the two ends joined by soldering.

Both the crown and the dome are curved in the shape of a cone while the skirt-band forms a circle. You will find the crown the most difficult component to form since it contains only eight pieces and more bending at each cross lead is required. To facilitate bending, apply a little heat to the leads by holding under a heat lamp or hot water.

Before attempting to join the two ends of any component, check the final cross lead channel and the ends of the perimeter leads to make sure the channel is free to receive the glass end. If some solder has run into the channel, it will be necessary to reheat and remove the excess solders or to replace the end cross lead if the blockage is excessive.

Trim off the excess perimeter leads before attempting to solder the final joints. On the end containing the final cross lead, cut the perimeter leads flush with the outside edge of the cross leads. On the end containing the exposed glass edge, cut the perimeter leads back at a slight angle leaving about 1/16 inch of the glass exposed—just enough to fit slightly into the opposite cross lead (Fig. 2-36). It may be necessary to overbend the component in order to bring the two ends into proper position for soldering.

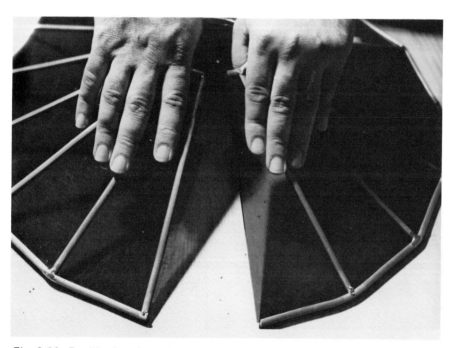

Fig. 2-36. Positioning dome for joining.

The assembly of the three components requires first joining the final dome to the skirt-band. Position both components as shown in Fig. 2-37. Cross leads should be aligned at each point of contact around the circumference. Since the components are not completely rigid until joined to one another, they may be formed or molded slightly for better alignment of the cross leads. When you are satisfied with the alignment, solder each of the 16 points of contact on the inside of the lamp (Fig. 2-38). Finally,

Fig. 2-37. Positioning assembled skirt-band component and dome for soldering.

Fig. 2-38. Soldering components at cross leads.

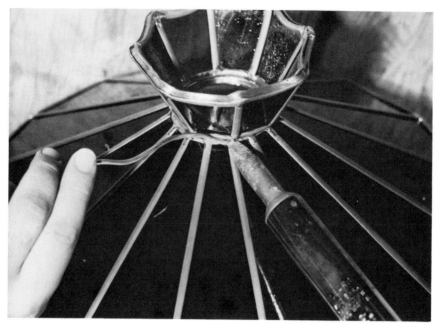

Fig. 2-39. Attaching crown to dome.

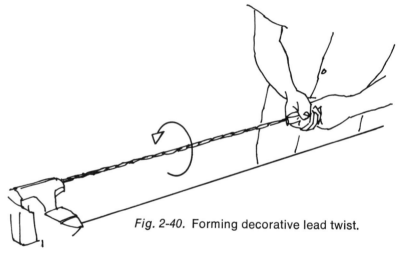

Fig. 2-40. Forming decorative lead twist.

the crown is joined to the dome by lightly soldering on the outside along the points of contact with the dome (Fig. 2-39).

A decorative lead twist will add to the esthetic value of the lamp by hiding the seams where components have been joined. To form a lead twist, secure one end of a lead strip in the bench vise and hold the opposite end with the pliers; stretch as shown in Fig. 2-40. Instead of removing the strip, begin twisting in one direction until the desired twist is obtained. Cut off the crushed

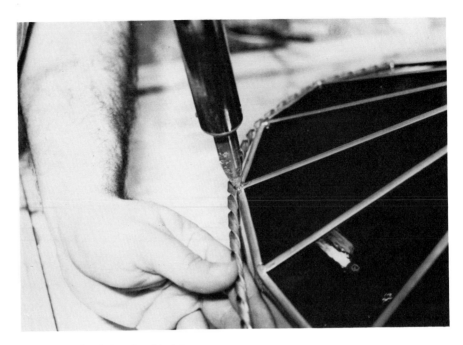

Fig. 2-41. Applying lead twist.

end of the lead twist with a knife. Using only the tip of the solder-ing iron, lightly solder the end of the lead twist to one of the cross leads directly over the seam (Fig. 2-41). Continue soldering the lead twist to each of the 16 cross leads. Trim all the excess care-fully at the point where both ends meet. Use the remaining piece to cover the seam between the dome and crown.

HANGING AND WIRING FOR ELECTRICAL OPERATION

Two methods, the swag and ceiling junction box, are commonly used to hang and wire the Tiffany-style and other suspended fixtures.

Electrical parts for hanging suspended fixtures are available in a variety of sizes and finishes. The material and description in Fig. 2-42 are used when the lamp is to be suspended from a ceil-ing junction box (Fig. 2-43). If the swag method (Fig. 2-44) is used, substitute an extra-long chain for the canopy set and fasten to the ceiling with hooks.

All materials are easily obtainable from most electrical supply or lamp specialty stores. If the lamp is to be suspended using

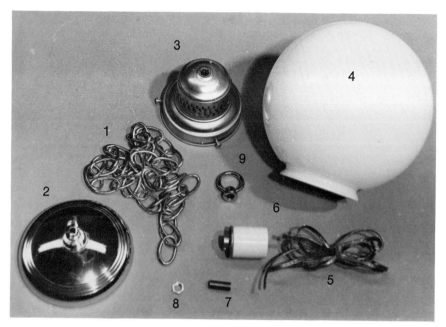

Fig. 2-42. Lamp parts for electrical operation.

Equipment Needed for Hanging Finished Lamp
(Fig. 2-42)

1. One yard fixture chain
2. Canopy set
3. Globe holder (3¼-inch fitter)
4. Glass globe (with 3¼-inch lip)
5. Four feet of lamp wire
6. Porcelain socket (keyless type)
7. One-inch threaded lamp pipe
8. Brass nut (to fit threaded pipe)
9. Hanging loop (threaded to fit lamp pipe)

the swag method, you can save money by purchasing all necessary wire, chain, and ceiling hooks in kit form.

Regardless of the method used, make certain that the weight of the lamp is supported entirely by the chain rather than the wire. Leave a slight bulge in the wire where the chain is attached

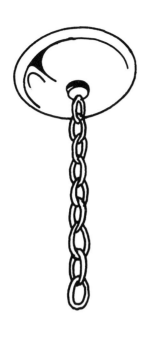

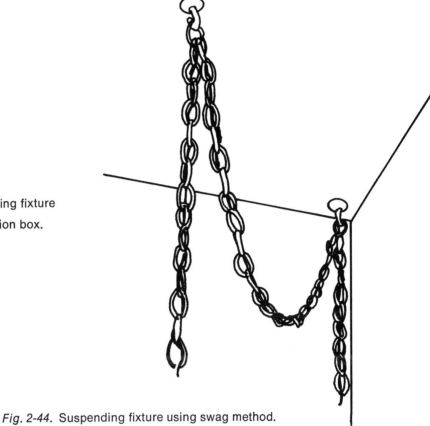

Fig. 2-43. Suspending fixture from a ceiling junction box.

Fig. 2-44. Suspending fixture using swag method.

to the hanging loop but do not loop or knot the wire itself since this practice will result in heat build-up and a short circuit.

Where the local electrical code requires grounded electrical fixtures, a third wire used as a ground should be attached to the metal part of the lamp and to the grounded ceiling junction box or grounded outlet.

3

LAMP STYLE
AND SIZE
VARIATIONS

The modern Tiffany-style lamp has been used to illustrate some of the basic processes of stained-glass crafting and to assist you in the construction of an item very much in demand for its beauty as well as its utility.

All of the basic techniques that you learned will be helpful in constructing lamps, windows, and other projects requiring your own creativity. With some simple modifications discussed below, virtually any style lamp can be made to suit your individual decor and taste.

Varying the Angle, Number of Pieces, and Components

Variations in the angle at which the glass is cut and the number of pieces contained in a lamp will produce a wide variety of shapes and sizes.

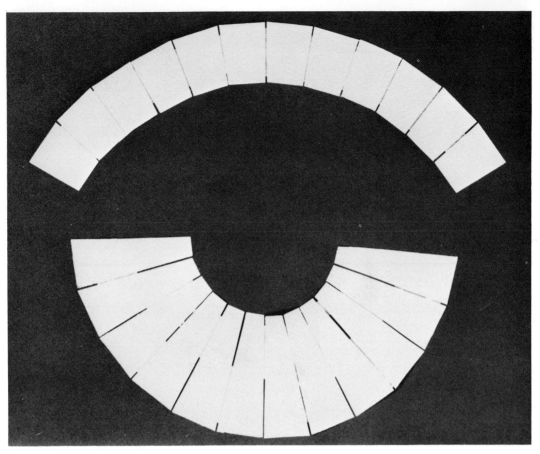

Fig. 3-1. Cardboard mock-up components.

A full-scale mock-up of the design you have in mind should first be constructed by cutting out pieces from heavy paper and taping them together where lead cames are ordinarily used. Spacing between each piece should be provided to allow for the 1/16-inch lead heart. A mock-up of each component should be made and all components assembled using adhesive tape (Fig. 3-1).

If the mock-up does not coincide with the idea you have in mind, you can increase or decrease its size or change the shape of any component by varying the angle of the individual pieces. To decrease the angle of the lower component of the paper mock-up in Fig. 3-2, change the angle of each piece from A to B (Fig. 3-3), and reassemble the component. The reconstructed mock-up using a decreased angle is shown in Fig. 3-4.

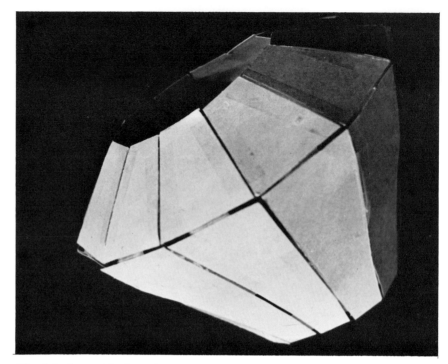

Fig. 3-2. Assembled mock-up.

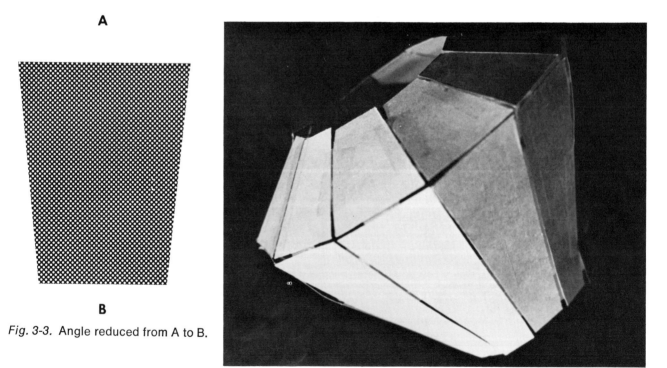

A

B

Fig. 3-3. Angle reduced from A to B.

Fig. 3-4. Reconstructed mock-up.

56

The paper mock-up serves to provide a visual simulation of the lamp prior to its actual construction, and the heavy paper used in the mock-up will serve as templates for setting the jig.

When you are satisfied with the mock-up, you are ready to begin cutting the necessary glass pieces. Remove one paper template, place in the ruler jig, and establish the angle as shown in Fig. 3-5.

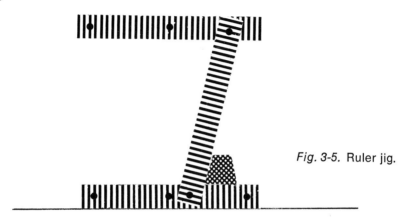

Fig. 3-5. Ruler jig.

Multiple-Level Suspended Fixtures

Stained-glass fixtures provide the unique flexibility in lighting that complements almost any decor. When you want to emphasize height, for example, several small lamps may be "stair-stepped" by suspending them from a spreader bar at various levels (Fig. 3-6).

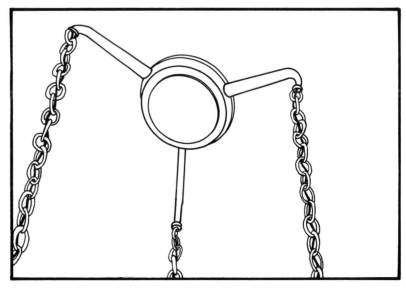

Fig. 3-6. Spreader bar for suspending fixtures.

All of the lamps shown in Fig. 3-7 are identical in size and shape and consist of only a 12-piece skirt and dome. Follow the same procedures outlined for the Tiffany-style lamp in Chapter 2. Templates are provided below for setting the ruler jig (Figs. 3-8 and 3-9).

Fig. 3-7. Multiple-level suspended fixtures.

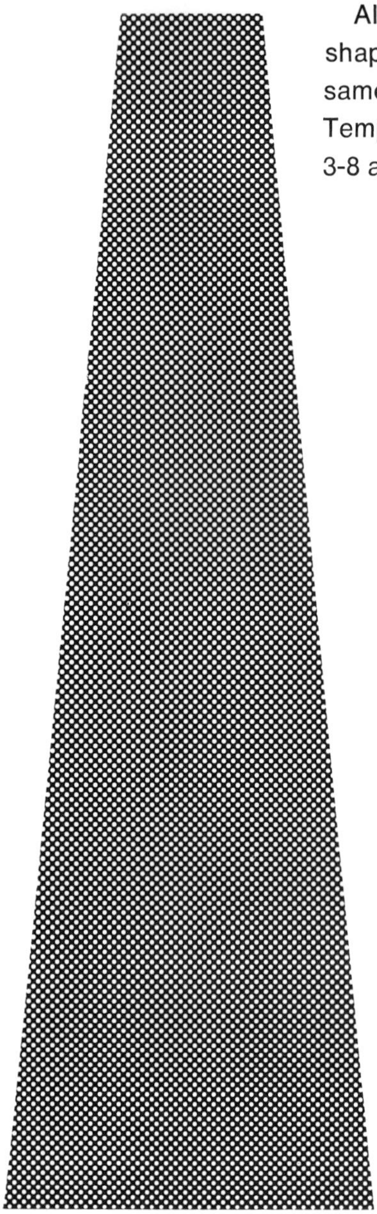

Fig. 3-8. Template for upper component of suspended fixture.

Fig. 3-9. Template for lower component of suspended fixture.

Fig. 3-10. Three-component suspended fixture.

Outdoor Lighting Using Stained Glass

Stained glass need not be limited only to indoor use since residential night lighting has aroused much interest in recent years. The outside of the home, in fact, offers many opportunities where lighting may be used creatively.

Ordinary fixtures often are not a welcome addition to the landscape during the day. Decorative fixtures made of stained glass can be used to add an accent to the landscape during the day and to provide the unique charm of subdued color at night.

Stained-glass lighting has been used successfully to light paths, walkways, driveways, and garden areas. Both functional and attractive, outdoor stained-glass fixtures will add to the beauty and value of your property.

Outdoor fixtures using stained glass can be as simple as an inverted cone, secured by brass fittings, and wired for electrical operation or somewhat more elaborate (Fig. 3-10). The lights shown in Figs. 3-11 and 3-12 consist of only 12 pieces to form the basic conical shape, using the templates pictured in Figs. 3-13 and 3-14 respectively.

Fixtures may be either portable or permanently installed. Driveway and walkway lights are not likely to be moved and can be permanently installed using underground cable. Prior to any underground installation, local electrical codes should be consulted for proper cable size and depth. Special-effects lighting for the garden or patio may be wired with a grounded plug and moved to any outside area equipped with an electrical supply.

Fig. 3-11. Permanently installed outdoor driveway light.

Fig. 3-13. Template for outdoor driveway light.

Fig. 3-12. Portable outdoor garden light.

Fig. 3-14. Template for outdoor garden light.

Fig. 3-15. Lighting for large rectangular worktable.

Special Effects Lighting

Many of the problems of lighting difficult areas may be solved by using stained-glass fixtures. Commercial fixtures may be unattractive or too expensive to be used in meeting special home lighting requirements. The fixture shown in Fig. 3-15 was designed to produce high light output over a large rectangular worktable. Basic construction is that of a four-sided box open at the top and bottom. Each half consists of four separate sides soldered together at the corners (Fig. 3-16).

The inverted top half is simply a smaller version of the bottom. The top dimensions of the bottom half and the bottom dimensions of the top half must be identical if the two parts are to join properly. Although each side of the lamp in Fig. 3-16 is divided

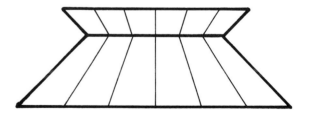

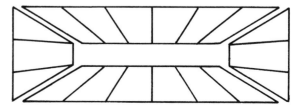

Fig. 3-16. Side and top views of Fig. 3-15.

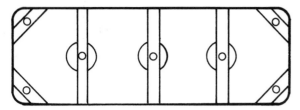

Fig. 3-17. Steel reinforcing structure for Fig. 3-15.

into a number of smaller sections, each side may consist of only one piece of glass if color simplicity is desired.

Large lamps will require special reinforcement. To provide rigidity and support when hanging, construct a rectangular frame using a steel reinforcing bar to form the outer perimeter and cross bars for attaching electrical sockets and chains. The supporting structure shown in Fig. 3-17 should fit snugly inside the lamp where the two components join. Solder the frame securely to the lamp where the frame and lead joints meet. Attach porcelain sockets to the diagonal cross bars using threaded lamp pipe, nuts, and chains.

Parts for Outdoor Fixture (Fig. 3-18)

1. Brass finial
2. Brass vase cap (8-inch)
3. Threaded lamp pipe—2 inch (⅛-IP)
4. Cross bar—4 inch (⅛-IP)
5. Threaded rod—8 inch (3/16-inch)
6. Nut (3/16-inch)
7. Keyless porcelain socket
8. Stained glass cone
9. Brass nut (⅛-IP)
10. Brass vase cap (3¼-inch)
11. Threaded lamp pipe—2 inch (⅛-IP)
12. Reducing bushing (½-inch–⅛-inch)
13. Steel pipe (threaded ½-inch)
14. Aluminum outdoor junction box
15. "L" connector
16. Outdoor grounded wire and plug
17. Grounded receptacle
18. Aluminum cover plate

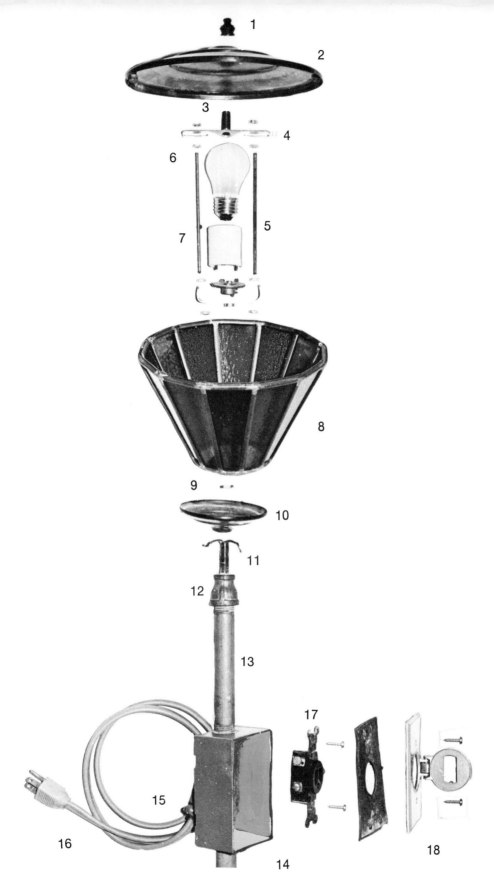

Fig. 3-18. Outdoor lighting fixture for portable or permanent installation.

63

4

THE MODERN STAINED-GLASS WINDOW

The Cartoon

The starting point of any stained-glass window is the conceptual design that may be only a rough sketch or a detailed full-color artist's drawing (Fig. 4-1). In either case you will want to translate the sketch or drawing into a full-sized working drawing known as the "cartoon" (Fig. 4-2).

The photostatic method may be used to enlarge the sketch to a full-sized cartoon, but this often proves too costly. More economical for the home craftsman is a method of redrawing a proportionately larger sketch several times the size of the original drawing. This requires the drawing of squares on the original sketch with an equal number of proportionately larger squares drawn on the cartoon paper. The design is then transferred square-by-square to the cartoon. To save the time used in drawing squares, you may want to purchase artist grid sheets containing preprinted squares.

Fig. 4-1. Sketch.

Fig. 4-2. Cartoon.

65

The Cutline

When the cartoon has been completed, two full-sized traced duplicates will be needed—one for a leading guide and the other for paper templates. The two copies can be made in one step by inserting carbon paper between each cartoon paper with the cartoon placed on top for tracing. Tape or tack all layers together to prevent movement during tracing.

Before tracing, study the diagram in Fig. 4-3 showing the lines that are to be traced from the cartoon.

Line A—the outer edge of the perimeter lead

Line B—the inner edge of the 1/16-inch heart of the perimeter lead

Line C—the inner edge of the perimeter lead

Line D—the exact center of the 1/16-inch heart of the inner lead

Using a sharp-pointed lead pencil, trace lines A, B, C, and D onto the traced cartoons. Use a straight edge wherever straight lines are indicated. When tracing line B, make certain that you are tracing only the inner edge of the lead heart. Line D requires a traced line in the center of the lead heart. Line A, of course, will mark the outer perimeter of the window. Number each section according to the relative position and the color of glass to be used. Remove traced paper and place on the workbench for a leading guide.

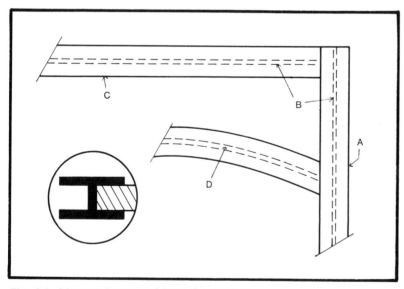

Fig. 4-3. Lines to be traced from the cartoon.

Paper Patterns

Most stained-glass studios use a professional double-blade pattern scissors that will remove a strip of paper to match exactly the width of the lead heart. Because this instrument is expensive and difficult to obtain, a makeshift device is recommended. Fig. 4-4 shows two single-edged razor blades separated by a small piece of wood and secured by a bolt. The separator should be of sufficient size to cause a 1/16-inch separation between the two blades to match the width of the lead heart. In addition to the double-blade cutter, you will need a separate single-edged blade or sharp knife for cutting the single line.

The double-blade cutter will be used only for Line D, representing the lead heart which separates the adjacent glass pieces. To use the cutter, center Line D between the two blades and carefully remove the entire black line (Fig. 4-5). You can expect a reasonably good cutting job by using the cutter edge and drawing the blades toward the bottom edge of the worktable. Cut Line B with a single blade since there will be no glass in the opposite channel. When lines B and D have been cut, you will have paper patterns to use in cutting the glass pieces to their exact size and shape. As each pattern is cut, mount it on a vertical clear glass

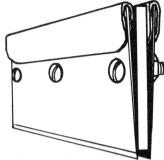

Fig. 4-4. Simple double-blade cutter.

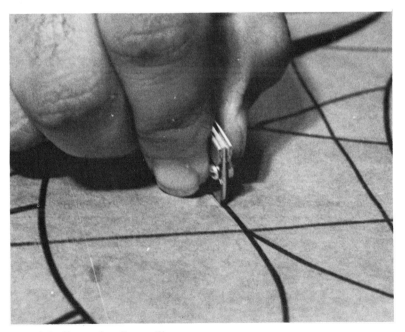

Fig. 4-5. Removing the cutline.

viewing screen with a small piece of double-stick tape. When mounting, be sure to allow for the 1/16-inch lead line space between patterns in order to avoid distortion in the design.

Some craftsmen prefer to trace lead lines onto the reverse side of the viewing screen to prevent light from passing through. Although this step will more closely simulate the final product, the additional time required to paint on lead lines is probably not worth the benefit it brings.

Cutting Glass to Pattern

The same basic technique of glass cutting described in preceding sections will be followed in glass cutting for the stained-glass window.

Cutting glass shapes to pattern requires practice in holding the cutter wheel close to the edge of the pattern (Fig. 4-6). You should strive to cut exactly to pattern, as even a slight deviation can cause the design not to conform to the cartoon. Remove each paper pattern from the viewing screen as each piece of glass is cut. Hold the pattern over the glass and maintain its position with the left hand. As each score is made, break off the excess immediately (Fig. 4-7). The cut piece should replace the pattern on

Fig. 4-6. Cutting glass to the pattern.

Fig. 4-7. Breaking at the score line.

the viewing screen (Fig. 4-8). Most studios use hot beeswax applied to the corners with an ordinary eye dropper to attach the cut glass to the viewing screen. A somewhat less messy method is to use small pieces of unheated beeswax sandwiched between the two glass pieces (Fig. 4-9).

Fig. 4-8. Cut glass pieces replacing paper patterns.

Fig. 4-9. All glass attached to the viewing screen.

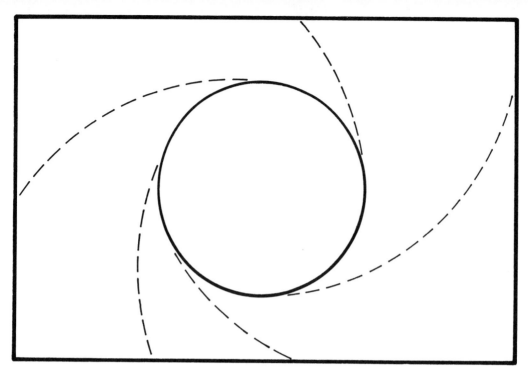

Fig. 4-10. Method for cutting a glass circle.

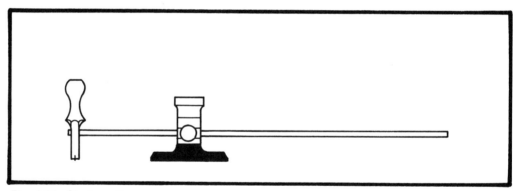

Fig. 4-11. Circle cutter.

When making a circular cut, do not attempt to remove the circle with a single score. Make a series of scores and break away one section at a time (Fig. 4-10). A circle cutter is a useful and inexpensive device to facilitate scoring circles varying from a few inches to four or more feet in diameter (Fig. 4-11).

The type of cut shown in Fig. 14, Chapter 2, can sometimes be made by scoring the semicircle and tapping the underside along the score line (Fig. 15, Chapter 2). If a deeper semicircular cut is desired, several scores and smaller cuts can be made until the proper size is obtained (Fig. 4-12). Often, however, the cut does not fracture properly, leaving pieces that must be removed. This is accomplished by nipping at the excess glass with the tip of the pliers, taking off small pieces at a time. Traditionally, this process is known as "grozing" (Fig. 4-13).

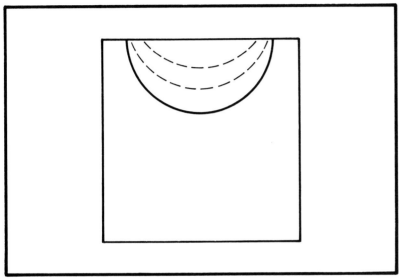

Fig. 4-12. Method for cutting a glass semicircle.

Fig. 4-13. Grozing with pliers.

Using Decorative Inserts

Decorative handspun roundels can make a positive contribution to the modern stained-glass window. Roundels not only produce a unique depth of color, but the high irregular center also makes for an interesting diversion from the typically flat surface.

Roundels are easily inset by making paper patterns that conform to the outer circle of the roundel. Lead lines of 1/16 inch should, of course, be provided between the roundel and patterns. Since roundels are handmade and vary from an exact circle, a wider lead of ⅝ or ½ inch is recommended around the perimeter to cover any irregular places on the glass. Solder the joint in the circular lead to one of the four intersecting leads (Fig. 4-14).

Using Zinc Cames

When additional strength is needed, zinc may be substituted for lead cames. Since zinc cannot be bent to conform to curvilinear cuts, its use is limited to straight geometric design or the outside perimeter of leaded glass windows. Zinc cames may be cut with a hacksaw or a power saw equipped with a metal cutting blade.

Fig. 4-14. Soldering joint to intersecting lead.

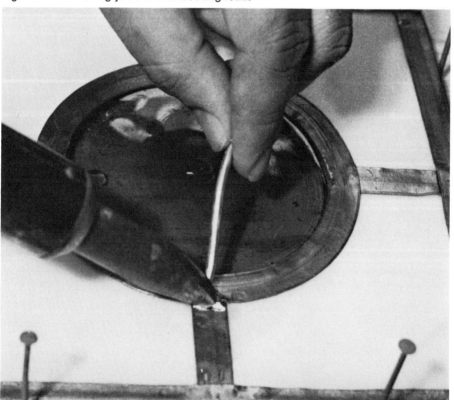

Fig. 4-15. Partially assembled window.

Assembly

For window assembly, the worktable must be equipped with straight wooden strips along the bottom and left edges, sufficient in length to match the dimensions of the window.

Tape or tack the traced leading guide to the surface of the worktable so the bottom and left traced perimeter leads are contiguous to the wooden support strips. Begin assembly of the window by placing the two perimeter leads in their proper position as shown by the leading guide. The first piece of glass should be placed in the corner where the two leads intersect (Fig. 4-15). Always make certain that the glass fits snugly into the lead channel, but avoid forcing the glass. If you encounter difficulty, run the blunt end of a lead pencil through the channel to widen the opening. A specially designed wooden tool known as a "lathkin" is often used for widening lead channels. A gentle tap with a wooden block held against the edge of the glass will cause a better seating of the lead and glass. This should be repeated often during the assembly process.

Choose a lead size that is appropriate to the design and provides a good balance between the lead and glass areas. In larger windows a lead size larger than the ¼ inch used in lamp construction is recommended. If you are having difficulty cutting glass exactly to pattern, a large lead will also serve to cover many of the cutting imperfections.

Where wide flat leads intersect, the edges should be slightly tucked under whenever possible (Fig. 4-16). Round leads should be cut as closely as possible (Fig. 4-17), and any minute gaps remaining will be filled in by soldering.

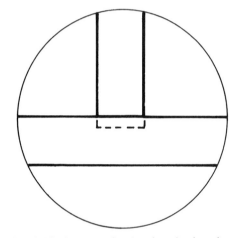

Fig. 4-16. Intersecting lead tucked under.

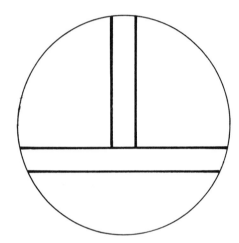

Fig. 4-17. Butting round leads.

Although professional craftsmen generally use a special weighted knife for cutting lead, any sharp retractable knife can be used effectively. A slight rocking back and forth motion of the knife rather than heavy pressure will help to keep the lead channel from being crushed during cutting.

When all leads have been arranged around the glass pieces, place the remaining two perimeter leads on the top and right edges of the window.

Reinforcing

A window of more than 3 feet in length should be reinforced with galvanized steel bars to prevent buckling and glass break-

Fig. 4-18. Soldering reinforcing bar.

age. Depending upon size, solder on reinforcing bars about every two feet. Bars should be soldered perpendicular to the surface of the window at any point that is likely to provide the best support and at the same time be least conspicuous. Wherever cross leads contact a reinforcing bar, solder both sides of each reinforcing bar to the intersecting leads (Fig. 4-18).

Sealing or Weatherproofing

One last step must be taken if the window is to be exposed to the elements. Although the glass may appear to be sealed by the lead cames, an exterior window will require further sealing.

An easy method of providing a weatherproof seal is to force putty between the glass and lead on both sides of the window. Grey or black putty will blend well with the lead cames and will be almost unnoticeable when the excess putty is removed.

5

FACETED GLASS

Purpose and Use

Only during the last several decades has faceted glass come into fashion as a new and distinct type of stained glass. To a considerable extent, faceted glass has rivaled the traditional method in the degree of interest shown in both religious and nonreligious works.

Faceted glass is the use of glass in its purest form without painting or surface staining. In a sense, faceted glass represents a return to the true nature of stained glass—the use of the medium itself as the source of beauty.

The Renaissance concept of the home translated into faceted glass is shown in Fig. 5-1. As the central theme, beautification of the home at night as viewed by the observer on the outside is as important as the view from the inside. Emphasis on movement as opposed to the static is achieved through the polarity of color and the explosive characteristics of the design itself.

Fig. 5-1. Faceted glass.

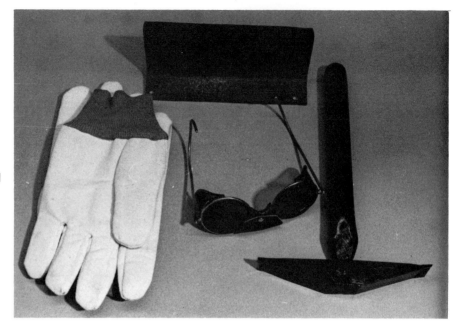

Fig. 5-2. Faceted glass tools.

Materials and Equipment (Fig. 5-2)

1. Slab glass (dalles)
2. Epoxy resin and hardener
3. ¾-inch framing strips
4. Waxed paper
5. Tempered steel anvil or large cold chisel
6. Tempered steel hammer
7. Protective goggles
8. Protective gloves
9. Rubber roller
10. Construction paper
11. Carbon paper
12. Chalk or white crayon
13. Grease
14. Wallpaper cleaner

Designs and Patterns

Designing in faceted glass should be kept to simple basic shapes because of unique problems in cutting slab or dalle glass. The initial design should be drawn on black construction paper with lines clearly separating the glass forms from the epoxy resin that will be poured around the glass. White chalk or crayon will show well against the black paper.

While faceted glass allows maximum freedom of design, some caveats are in order. To maximize strength, there should be a balance between the glass and epoxy. When there is an uneven distribution, differences in expansion and contraction between the glass and epoxy become intensified. Designing in faceted glass, therefore, should strive to achieve a proper balance for maximum strength.

To execute the design, place carbon paper, carbon side up, on the worktable. Over the carbon place a layer of waxed paper and tack or tape along the edges to prevent movement. Position the drawing that you made on black construction paper over the waxed paper surface and trace over the white lines with a pen or pencil (Fig. 5-3). When all lines have been traced, remove the construction paper. You will notice that the design has been lightly traced on the underside of the waxed paper and should be visible if sufficient pressure has been applied in tracing. Cut out glass templates from the construction paper design and use as templates for cutting and shaping the glass pieces.

Fig. 5-3. Sketch drawn on black construction paper.

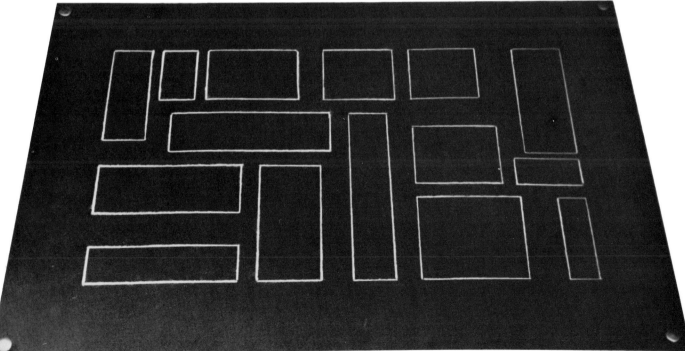

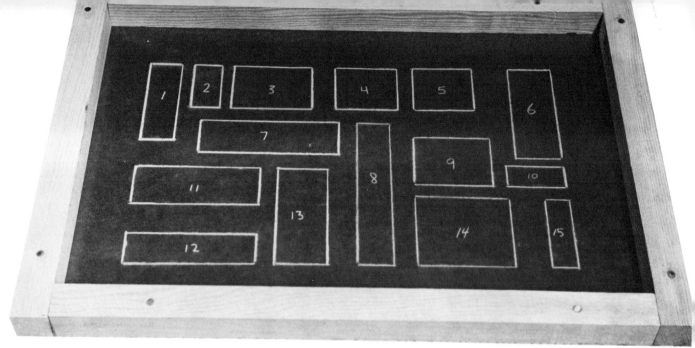

Fig. 5-4. Sketch with framing strips.

The Work Area

The same worktable used for leaded glass may be used for faceted glass; however, the table must be perfectly level to avoid variations in thickness when the epoxy resin is poured. After the design has been traced, nail wood framing strips over the edges of the waxed paper, making sure that there are no wrinkles that may result in an uneven surface appearance (Fig. 5-4). Using a rubber roller, coat the entire waxed paper surface and the inside surfaces of the wood framing strips with transparent grease, such as Orange Solid Oil. Only a thin layer is needed to act as a release agent for the epoxy. The design should be visible through the layer of grease if properly applied (Fig. 5-5).

Fig. 5-5. Applying transparent grease.

Cutting the Dalle

Assuming that the design will require pieces about one-fourth the size of an 8″ x 12″ dalle, make the first cut by scoring the dalle across the middle on the smooth shiny side (Fig. 5-6). Using the anvil or the supported cold chisel, bring the dalle down over the cutting directly under the score line (Fig. 5-7). Even though the dalle is considerably thicker than other types of stained glass, only slightly more pressure is required to cause separation. When the dalle has been cut in half, score each half in the middle across the width and repeat the breaking procedure. Any piece smaller than one-quarter of a dalle will likely require chipping down to the desired size and shape. Use the paper templates that were cut previously as guides for chipping to the correct size.

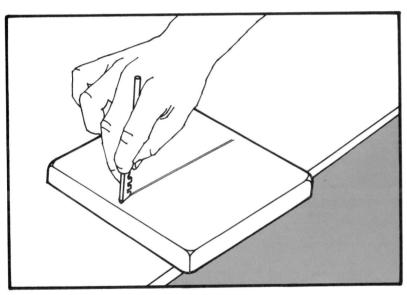

Fig. 5-6. Scoring the dalle.

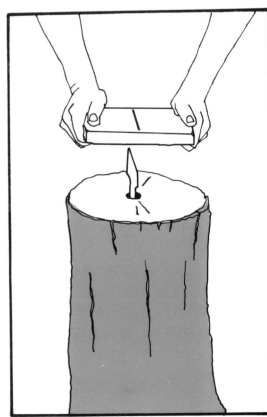

Fig. 5-7. Breaking the dalle over a cold chisel.

Chipping and Faceting

Chipping is required after cutting when the dalle is to be shaped or reduced further in size. Fig. 5-8 shows the technique used for removing excess glass. Note that the glass is held against the anvil while striking. Only practice will provide the experience necessary to know the correct angle of strike and the right amount of pressure. Practice on scrap pieces is strongly recommended before projects are actually begun.

Faceting adds considerable luster and brilliance to the glass and is, of course, the hallmark of faceted glass. The amount of faceting is strictly a matter of personal preference. Some craftsmen use faceting sparingly while others facet the entire surface area. Faceting should be restricted to the rough or interior face only, since faceting the exterior surface would result in the epoxy running under the glass and blocking the passage of light. Protective gloves and goggles should be worn at all times while chipping and faceting to avoid hand and eye injuries.

To facet, hold the dalle, shiny side up, in the left hand and strike on the edge about one-quarter of the way down from the rough face (Fig. 5-9). The broken piece will separate, leaving a smooth swirllike impression along the edge and rough face.

Before pouring the epoxy, you will want to preview the window to measure the color effect against the original design. Using the cut-out black construction paper and a light box, place each piece of glass into its respective space in the cut-out. The black

Fig. 5-8. Chipping.

Fig. 5-9. Faceting.

Fig. 5-10. Applying grease.

Fig. 5-11. Placing pieces in position over the sketch.

spaces, of course, simulate the epoxy areas where the passage of light is eliminated.

As each piece of glass is cut and faceted, spread a thin layer of grease (Fig. 5-10) over the entire smooth, nonfaceted surface and place directly over the pattern outline (Fig. 5-11). Be sure that no grease has become smeared on the edges of the glass, since epoxy will not adhere to greasy or oily surfaces.

Casting

When faceted glass was first introduced, concrete reinforced with steel wires was the only matrix available for setting the glass. Cracking and loose glass were inevitable problems due to expansion differentials between the glass and surrounding concrete. With the development of epoxies, these problems have been largely resolved. Epoxy resin consists of two parts—a catalyst and hardening agent—that produce a chemical reaction when combined. When allowed to harden properly, epoxy forms a strong permanent bond.

83

Epoxy resin is available from most suppliers in gallon quantities in a variety of colors. Each supplier includes specific instructions for combining the catalyst and hardener and curing time under proper temperature conditions. As a rule of thumb, one gallon of epoxy resin will be enough for about three square feet of area cast ⅝ inch deep. This will, of course, vary according to the amount of glass used as well as the depth of the cast.

Before casting, any low-faceted areas should be temporarily filled with wallpaper cleaner to prevent epoxy from flowing into the faceted area and blocking the passage of light.

The entire top of the gallon can may be removed with a can opener and used as a pouring spout. Add the separate container of hardener according to the manufacturer's instructions.

Casting at the correct temperature is the most critical factor in achieving a strong, long-lasting panel. Epoxy resins should never be heated above the recommended casting temperature in an attempt to achieve a faster flow. Overheating epoxy will cause a speed-up in the normal chemical reaction and result in undue stress. Conversely, epoxy that is too cold will be difficult to pour and slow to produce the necessary chemical reaction.

If mixed at the proper temperature, the epoxy should flow easily between all of the glass pieces (Fig. 5-12). A cast depth

Fig. 5-12. Pouring epoxy resin.

of ⅝ inch is recommended but variations between ½ and ¾ inch may occur depending on the strength desired. Two colors may be used jointly, such as charcoal on the exterior and mortar on the interior. Pour the exterior charcoal color first to about one-half the desired depth. When partially cured, pour the remaining thickness using the mortar color. To achieve a textured interior surface, sprinkle on white or colored sand or pebbles before the epoxy sets. If only the epoxy itself is used as the finished surface, you may notice small bubbles forming on the surface shortly after pouring. These may be removed without disturbing the epoxy by lightly spraying the surface with acetone.

Follow the manufacturer's instructions in allowing sufficient time for curing before moving the work. Normally, the panel should remain flat on the work surface for 48 hours. Again, proper temperature plays an important part during the curing as well as the mixing and pouring phase. Precaution should be taken to maintain the recommended temperature day and night during the curing time.

When properly cured, remove the molding strips and waxed paper, and remove grease from the exterior surface with acetone. If a little epoxy has run beneath the glass surface, carefully chip away the excess epoxy so all of the glass is visible.

6

COPPER FOIL

The Use of Copper Foil

The use of copper foil as a substitute for lead is not new. In fact, many of the early stained-glass lamps were made with copper foil strips rather than lead to secure the large number of small pieces of glass. Copper offers the distinct advantage of weight reduction which becomes an important consideration in the building of large suspended fixtures. In addition, copper produces an entirely different external appearance. The effect of age can be created immediately through a simple process, whereas lead requires a long period of time to react naturally to the elements.

Materials Needed

Copper foil is available in rolls in a variety of widths. The underside is pre-coated with adhesive for easy application to the glass surface. A width of ¼ inch is recommended for general use to provide both the necessary surface for soldering and a pleasing appearance.

Fig. 6-1. Copper foil materials.

Zinc chloride soldering flux, such as Rubyfluid, should be used since oleic acid will not react with copper and cannot be used.

Lastly, copper sulphate powder will be needed to produce the darker, aged appearance. This product is readily available in one-pound quantities from most drug store or pharmaceutical suppliers (Fig. 6-1).

Patterning Without Lead Lines

Cutting patterns is somewhat simpler when copper foil is used in place of the 1/16-inch lead line. When you have drawn a pattern, cut along the pattern line with a single-edged razor blade or scissors (Fig. 6-2). The small amount of additional space occupied by the foil will not markedly affect the alignment of the glass pieces.

Fig. 6-2. Cutting the pattern with a single-edged blade.

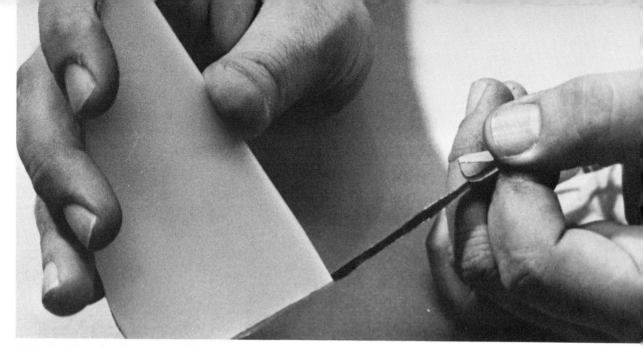

Fig. 6-3. Wrapping in copper foil.

Applying Copper Foil

Each glass piece must be wrapped in copper foil before assembly and soldering. Begin by unrolling several inches of foil and stripping off the protective backing. Center the edge of the glass onto the foil at any beginning point along the perimeter of the glass (Fig. 6-3). The final joint should overlap slightly where the two ends meet. Separate by cutting with a scissors or razor blade. Press the foil down firmly onto both faces of the glass and smooth with your fingernail to remove any wrinkles (Fig. 6-4). Assemble all pieces tightly and use small nails around the outer edge where needed to prevent shifting while soldering.

Fig. 6-4. Pressing the foil to the glass surface.

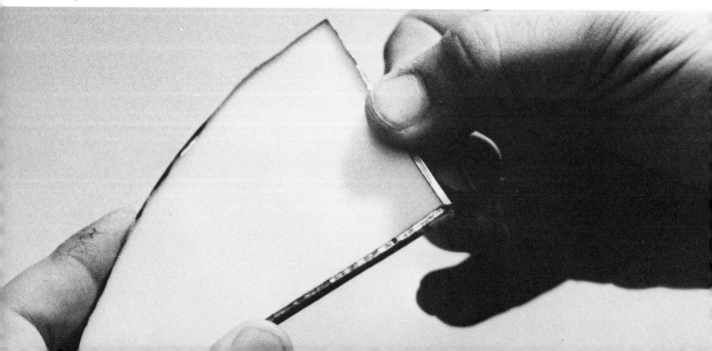

Soldering

When the glass pieces have been assembled, apply zinc chloride flux liberally with a small brush to all copper foil surfaces on the upper face. Long strands of solder should be used since smaller pieces tend to become hot quickly. When working with copper foil, solder is applied liberally to fill the crevice between adjoining pieces. Less consideration is given to temperature since copper melts at a much higher temperature than lead. However, caution should be exercised not to allow the soldering iron to remain at any one point for more than an instant. Heat generated by the iron and retained by the copper foil may result in glass breakage. Fig. 6-5 shows the procedure recommended for soldering copper foil. Hold the solder strip in the left hand, under and slightly to the front of the soldering tip. Draw the iron over the foil and toward the bottom edge of the worktable. The solder will flow smoothly onto the copper foil, filling in most of the gaps between adjoining pieces. It is important that all exposed copper surfaces be coated with solder in order for the copper sulphate to react properly. With a little practice you will learn to feed the solder while continuously moving the soldering tip over the joints.

When all joints have been soldered, remove all holding nails, reverse the work, and solder the opposite face in the same manner.

Fig. 6-5. Soldering.

Fig. 6-6. Rubbing the soldered area with copper sulphate.

Applying Copper Sulphate

Remove all traces of flux with scouring powder or detergent. Wearing protective gloves, sprinkle a small amount of copper sulphate powder onto a damp rag and rub all metal surfaces. You will immediately notice a change in color from silver to dark copper (Fig. 6-6). Additional applications of copper sulphate will produce darker shades of copper color. When the desired appearance has been attained, clean by holding the work under water to remove excess copper sulphate.

Some Simple Projects

JEWELRY BOX

A colorful box for cigarettes, jewelry, and other ornaments can be constructed by soldering together panels of glass wrapped in foil (Fig. 6-7). Solder the four sides together on both the inside and outside corners. The bottom panel should then be cut to match the outer perimeter of the glass sides. A hinged lid may be added by soldering miniature hinges to the edge of one of the vertical panels (Fig. 6-8).

SAILS

The same basic techniques are followed in making a group of stained-glass sails (Fig. 6-9). Color selection becomes an impor-

Fig. 6-7. Copper foil boxes.

STEPHAN HEISE

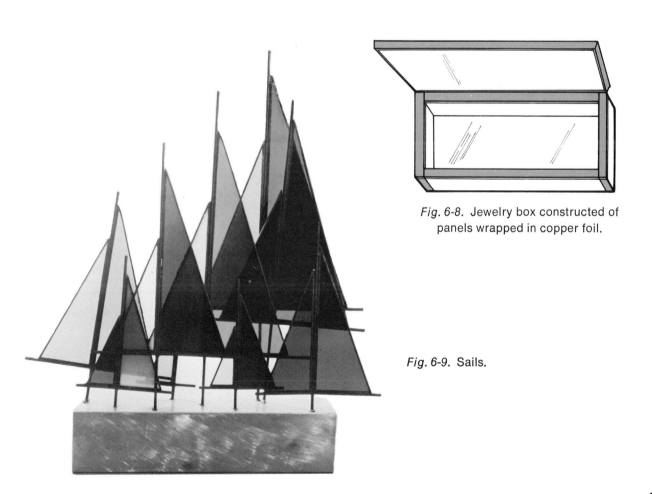

Fig. 6-8. Jewelry box constructed of panels wrapped in copper foil.

Fig. 6-9. Sails.

tant factor since overlapping sails of various colors of glass can produce very interesting color combinations. In addition to glass and foil, you will need 3/16-inch diameter brass rods for the upright and horizontal supports for each sail. A heavy block of wood or metal that can be drilled to accommodate the rods should be used as a base.

If you want each sail to have the same angle, the ruler jig set for an angular cut may be used (Fig. 6-10). When all glass sails have been cut and wrapped with foil, position metal rods, and secure with nails while soldering (Fig. 6-11). Follow the same procedure for soldering and applying copper sulphate powder.

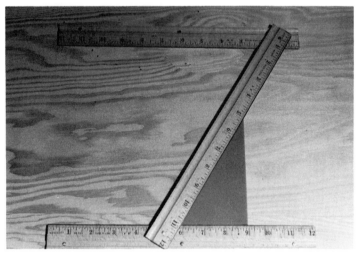

Fig. 6-10. Ruler jig set for cutting sails.

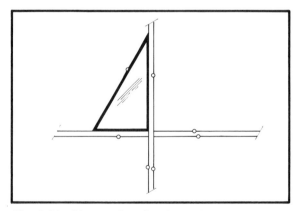

Fig. 6-11. Glass sail and rods positioned for soldering.

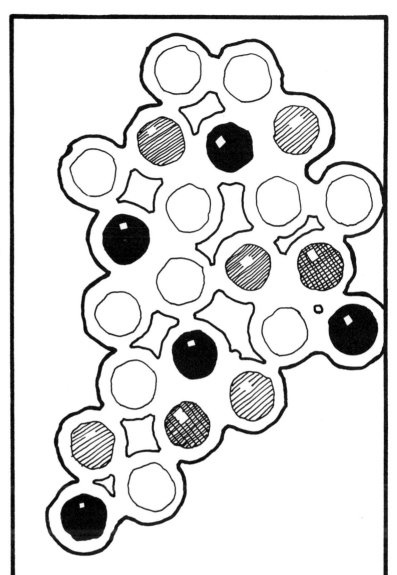

Fig. 6-12. Grape cluster.

GRAPE CLUSTER

Small glass globules or miniature roundels can be used as grapes in the construction of a stained-glass grape cluster. Begin by wrapping each glass piece in foil. Copper foil is particularly effective in this type of project since its dark color enhances the appearance of the glass. Arrange the group in a traditional grape cluster design leaving open spaces at random (Fig. 6-12). Two or three green glass leaves and a length of wire solder for the stem may be added.

7

TRACING AND PAINTING ON GLASS

Why Paint on Glass?

At first, it might appear unnecessary to apply paint to the surface of colored glass. Indeed, painting is the very process that led the craft down the path of demise during the sixteenth, seventeenth, and eighteenth centuries. Modern glass technology has provided the craft of stained glass with an almost infinite variety of colors in glass and would seem to have shut the door to the glass painter and his technique.

Painting on glass, however, does have its place in the twentieth century. In most modern stained-glass works, it takes a back seat position, acting as a means of accentuating the quality of the glass medium itself.

Through the application of tracing lines and matting color (painting) forms, shapes and textures are represented that could not otherwise be achieved with glass and lead alone (Fig. 7-1). Larger glass pieces with less lead work may be substituted for the tedious task of showing all detail through the use of lead

Fig. 7-1. Tracing and painting on glass.

lines. Tracing lines of various widths used in conjunction with lead also provide an effective means of expanding or emphasizing lead lines where opaque areas are desired. Color control is as important in stained glass as the proper use of lead lines. Matting color provides an excellent means of defining the degree of light and color projection. Some colors of glass are so strong that a halation effect may cause lead lines to become invisible. Tracing and matting colors applied intelligently can effectively control light and color to maintain a balanced relationship between the glass and lead.

Tracing on Glass

Tracing is the process of painting on lines which serve as part of the basic design. Three basic tracing methods are commonly used—commercial squeegie paste; the traditional method using tracing color, water, and gum; and heavy painting medium. The choice of methods is strictly a matter of personal preference. The commercial squeegie paste method provides a black opaque appearance when fired, while the other two add color to the tracing lines. The former is somewhat easier to use than the traditional method because it will not smear when matting color is applied in the second step. The heavy painting medium method produces a blend of material close to the squeegie paste effect yet is easier to use than the traditional. For this reason, it is more commonly used than the other two methods.

TRACING WITH COMMERCIAL SQUEEGIE PASTE

To prepare the necessary tracing blend, mix a small amount of prepared commercial squeegie paste with turpentine on a ground glass pallet (Fig. 7-2). When the mixture has attained the consistency of a light cream, it is ready to be applied directly to the glass.

TRACING WITH THE TRADITIONAL METHOD

Preparation of a tracing blend according to the traditional method requires the use of three ingredients—tracing color, gum arabic powder, and water. Tracing colors vary according to personal preference. A blend of black and brown tracing colors is most commonly used as a tracing preparation, but other colors are sometimes used depending on the result you wish to achieve.

Mix the two colors thoroughly on a ground glass pallet and add water a little at a time into a center depression of the mixture (Fig. 7-3). Enough water should be added to bring the blend to a light cream consistency.

Fig. 7-2. Mixing commercial squeegie paste and turpentine.

Fig. 7-3. Mixing matting colors and water.

Fig. 7-4. Grinding the mixture to a fine cream consistency.

Next, add water to the powdered gum arabic in a separate container and mix until the powder is in suspension. Add about a tablespoon of liquid gum arabic to the blend of matting colors and water, and continue to blend in all ingredients thoroughly. Most craftsmen prefer a finely ground blend to insure that materials do not separate during the firing period. A fine cream texture can be achieved by grinding the blend with a glass ball known as a "muller" shown in Fig. 7-4.

TRACING WITH HEAVY PAINTING MEDIUM

An often preferred tracing method consists of a mixture of tracing colors (black, brown, red, etc.) and heavy painting medium. Mix tracing colors and heavy painting medium at the ratio of four to one respectively, blending to a heavy cream consistency.

APPLYING TRACING COLOR

A light box consisting of a back-lighted clear glass screen is recommended for tracing and matting color applications. Place the full-sized cartoon on the surface of the light box and the glass piece to be traced in position over the cartoon. The light emanating from below should cause the tracing lines from the cartoon to be visible through the glass, providing a clear field for

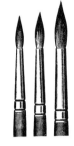

Fig. 7-5. Red sable
tracing brushes.

STEWART CLAY CO., INC.,
NEW YORK

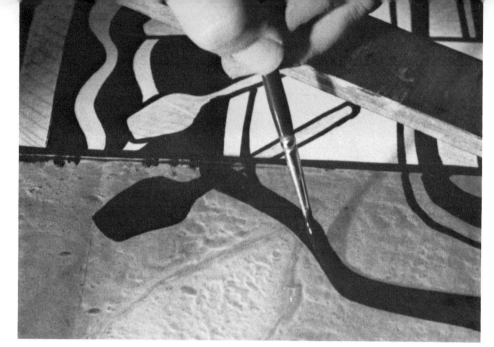

Fig. 7-6. Applying tracing lines.

the application of tracing lines. Most glass painters use a simple wooden device known as a bridge to support the forearm while tracing. The bridge consists of a narrow piece of wood with a vertical wooden support on each end.

Transfer the trace lines to the glass surface. Using a red sable brush (Figs. 7-5 and 7-6) or any other brush suitable to the size of the job, pick up enough tracing medium to produce the desired effect. Heavier lines, of course, require a greater quantity of paint. If a smooth tracing edge is preferred, rather than a distinct determinable line, use a small dry sponge to "stipple" or feather the edge. Lightly tap the surface of the wet tracing line until the desired blotting effect is achieved. Tracing lines should be allowed to dry thoroughly before matting color is applied. Under normal conditions, drying requires several hours depending on room temperature. Drying time can be reduced considerably by placing the glass in a kiln heated to about 200 degrees Fahrenheit.

Applying Matting Color

Preparation for matting color application or "painting" follows almost the same blending procedure as the traditional method of preparing a blend for tracing. In the matting blend, less gum arabic is normally used than in the preparation of the tracing mixture. The addition of gum in various amounts will lend to the adherence of the painting to the glass surface. The proportion of ingredients in the blend will vary considerably and will depend on personal preference and technique.

A blend of colors commonly used in stained-glass studios for matting application consists of two parts of bistro brown color to about one part grey green. Green alone will fire toward a black appearance without any perceptible color value. With the addition of brown, firing will cause a light brown cast.

Tracing lines applied in the previous operation must be allowed to dry thoroughly before matting color is applied to avoid smearing of the tracing lines.

Before applying matting color to the actual work, use a small piece of scrap glass to test for proper adherence and special matting variations you want to achieve. Matting color may be applied in a very thin veil of color or very deep, or any degree of density in between.

Apply matting color to the entire surface using a mottling brush (Fig. 7-7) in long even strokes (Fig. 7-8). Using a flat badger blender (Fig. 7-9), immediately stroke the painted surface lightly in opposite directions to remove all unwanted brush strokes (Fig. 7-10). When fired, glass will absorb a portion of the iron oxide and approximately 15 percent of the matting color will be lost, thereby adding to the translucency of the glass. Compensation for this loss may be made by applying slightly more matting color.

Fig. 7-7. Mottling brush.

STEWART CLAY CO., INC.,
NEW YORK

Fig. 7-8. Applying matting color.

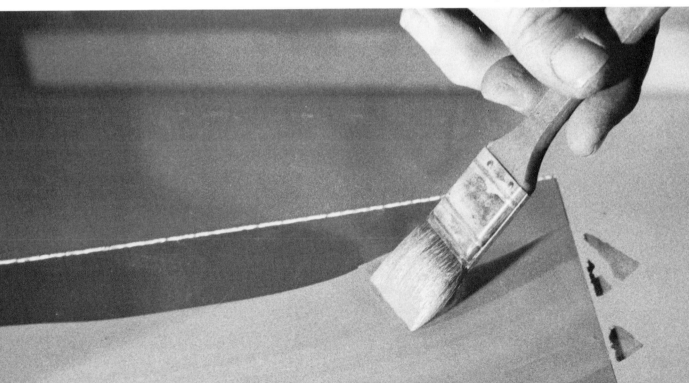

Fig. 7-9. Blender brush.

STEWART CLAY CO., INC.,
NEW YORK

Fig. 7-10. Smoothing out matting color.

Variations of Matting Applications

After the matting color has been applied and allowed to dry, one or more techniques may be used to control translucency and to create designs in the matting color surface. "Stippling" of the matting color (Fig. 7-11) is most often used to produce a softened effect. A special stippling brush (Fig. 7-12) may be used to lightly dab the surface. If a bolder stippling effect is desired, the badger blender may be used in the same manner as the stippling brush. Many interesting designs can be created by drawing the teeth of a comb across the surface or by using the palm

Fig. 7-12. Stippling brushes.

STEWART CLAY CO., INC.,
NEW YORK

Fig. 7-11. Stippling matting color.

Fig. 7-13. Using the palm of the hand to rub matting color.

Fig. 7-14. Using a paint brush for special effects.

of the hand to lightly rub out a portion of the color (Fig. 7-13). Other variations of the matting color can be created by mottling with crumpled cloth or paper or simply by drawing an ordinary paint brush across the surface (Fig. 7-14). The variations are limited only by one's imagination and creativity.

Firing

Firing of glass to produce the necessary chemical reaction requires a temperature of approximately 1220 degrees Fahrenheit. Temperature will vary somewhat according to the painting medium and the type of glass. A small inexpensive kiln will usually suffice where only small pieces of glass are fired individually (Fig. 7-15).

Some kilns are equipped with temperature gauges and may be timed for precise firing. Other smaller models have peep holes or ceramic cones which begin to melt when a specified temperature has been reached.

Painted glass should, however, be fired to the point where the glass becomes cherry red and the tracing and matting colors take on a shiny appearance. When the firing level has been reached, the kiln should be shut off and allowed to cool slowly.

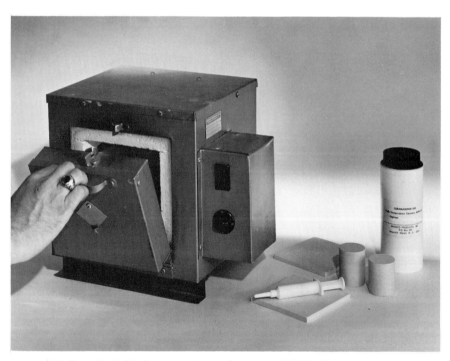

Fig. 7-15. Standard high-temperature furnace, 2150° F.

AREMCO PRODUCTS, INC., BRIARCLIFF MANOR, N.Y.

STAINED-GLASS MOSAIC

Historical Sketch

The history and development of mosaic poses a striking parallel to that of stained glass. Like stained glass, mosaic had its beginning in antiquity and was subject to many of the same conditions which have influenced the development of stained glass.

Several thousand years before the Christian era, mosaics were being used widely in architectural design and jewelry in the Middle East. Further development of mosaic took place during the Greek and Roman periods when glass and ceramics were used in conjunction with marble and stone as mosaic tesserae. It was in Rome where brightly colored glass known today as Byzantine or Italian glass was developed.

By the sixth century, mosaic became the handmaiden of the Church in spreading the Gospel. Between the sixth and eleventh centuries, mosaic reached its height in success. The Gothic mosaicists are known for their use of striking and vibrant colors as well as their knowledge of light and its effect upon the medium.

During the Renaissance, mosaic, like stained glass, was reduced largely to imitating the Italian murals in the great cathedrals. Striving to duplicate the detail of oil painting, the Renaissance mosaicist used smaller and smaller tesserae to achieve his desired goal. By mid-seventeenth century, the craft reached its lowest ebb. Emulation of the oil painter continued throughout much of the nineteenth century as Naturalism continued to be the dominant theme.

Contemporary works point to the revival of mosaic as a distinct art form. New materials and processes are being introduced and employed in architectural design, and craftsmen are using individual creativity and design to a much greater extent.

Many worthwhile projects can be undertaken using leftover pieces of glass from other projects. Glasses and vases are easily decorated with multi-colored glass tesserae, giving them old world charm. Larger projects such as coffee tables and wall murals can also be undertaken.

Method and Procedure

Either the direct or indirect method of making mosaics can be used. In the direct method, tesserae are cemented directly to the supporting surface; in the indirect method, the mosaic design is completed front face down and transferred to the support to which it will be glued.

In most cases transparent cement, such as Dupont Duco cement, will be needed to maintain the passage of light. Be certain that the glass is free of dirt or grease before gluing by cleaning it with denatured alcohol. Always allow sufficient time for the glue to harden before grouting.

Whenever small square or rectangular pieces of tesserae are required, you can use the ruler jig with a nail stop set for the desired size. If you are adept at using the glass cutter you might want to cut the tesserae freehand to achieve a rough, natural look. Glass globules or small roundels may be used in conjunction with cathedral glass to achieve a relief effect.

Grouting is the process of filling in spaces between the glass tesserae with a fine cementlike filler known as Tile Grout. Water should be stirred in a little at a time until the mixture is the consistency of heavy cream. With a rubber glove, spread the grout over the surface, working it into the crevices between the glass pieces. Remove excess grout with a damp sponge after the grout has had sufficient time to set. To avoid cracking, spray or wet the surface with a sponge several times during the drying period.

Grout may be tinted any color by the addition of powdered tempera paint, lamp black, or water base paint to the powdered grout before adding water. The amount of tint will, of course, depend on the intensity of the color that you want. A little experimentation with a small amount of grout will avoid disappointments when a larger amount is prepared for the actual project.

Instead of light passing through the tesserae and the supporting surface, you may want the light to be reflected from the supporting surface and back through the glass tesserae. Aluminum foil can be used over the supporting surface and immediately under the glass tesserae, adding considerable sparkle and depth to the already translucent quality of the glass. If the foil is wrinkled rather than smooth, the effect will be intensified.

Stained-Glass Mosaic Projects

COFFEE TABLE

Aluminum foil cemented to a strong wooden base provides an excellent reflective backing for a stained-glass coffee table. Transparent cement must be used liberally to prevent grout from seeping between the glass and foil. Make sure that the cement is squeezed out around the glass to seal the opening when the glass

Fig. 8-1. Mosaic coffee table.

is pressed into position. About ⅛ inch of space, to be filled with grout, should be allowed between the glass pieces. Variations in surface texture through the use of dissimilar materials can highlight the glass areas. Plaster of Paris, crushed stone, or even cement may be used in combination with glass (Fig. 8-1).

CANDLE HOLDER

Any goblet or brandy snifter can be decorated with small pieces of stained glass. Generally, glass pieces used around a curved surface should not exceed about ⅜ inch in width. If wider pieces are used, it may be difficult to maintain complete contact with the glass surface. Glass tesserae may be cut into small squares or rectangles or pieces may be cut to the full length of the object. Be sure to leave about ⅛ inch of space on the top and bottom as well as between the individual pieces for filling with grout (Fig. 8-2).

Fig. 8-2. Mosaic candle holders.

9

ADDITIONAL PROJECTS AND TECHNIQUES

Stained-Glass Ornaments

In recent years there has been an upsurge of interest in hanging or standing ornaments (Fig. 9-1). These items usually carry high price tags in retail stores, but they can be made easily and at a small fraction of their retail cost.

Here is an opportunity to exercise your own creativity. The design need not be complicated to achieve some interesting creations.

Use a single channel perimeter lead around the outside for a finished appearance and double channel such as ⅜″ or ¼″ H for all internal leads. You will need a basic design and paper patterns made from the original sketch so that space for lead lines is provided.

Always connect adjoining sections at the point where the ends of the perimeter leads have been soldered (Figs. 9-2 and 9-3). This makes for a neater job by minimizing the number of soldered connections.

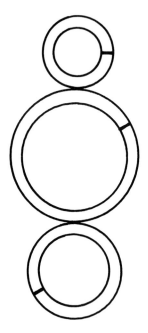

Fig. 9-1. Standing figures.

WILLIAM J. GERARD

Fig. 9-2. Incorrect positioning for soldering.

Fig. 9-3. Correct positioning for soldering.

Aciding

Flashed glass is essentially a double layer of glass made while the glass is in the molten state. Normally a "flash" of red, blue, or white, is made over clear glass, but other colors are sometimes available.

Any glass area exposed to a bath of hydrofluoric acid will be eroded by the action of the acid; areas covered by a protective coating will be free of erosion. Some craftsmen use the traditional method of painting hot beeswax on the flashed surface. The beeswax, acting as a stopping agent, will prevent the erosion of any flashed surface protected.

A much simpler "stopping" process is to use plastic tape or contact paper over the areas to be protected. To insure complete contact at the edges, the glass must be clear and dry and the tape firmly pressed to the glass surface.

Generally 48 percent hydrofluoric acid will be sufficent to produce the erosive action necessary. The time required depends on the thickness of the flash. Thinly flashed glass may require only a few minutes of contact with the acid while a heavily layered flash may take up to an hour. Brush on acid to the exposed glass areas and repeat until the flash is removed. (Fig. 9-4).

When erosion is completed, remove the glass and hold it under running water until all traces of acid have been removed.

Fig. 9-4. Applying hydrofluoric acid.

Laminating Glass

The bonding of multiple layers of glass together to achieve the desired color combination and three-dimensional effect has in recent years received a great deal of attention.

Commissions of both a religious and nonreligious nature have been carried out by Willet Studios in Philadelphia who imported the technique from Holland in 1965. The process, patented under the trade name "Farbigem" (Figs. 9-5 and 9-6), uses a secret gluing process far stronger than epoxy type glues.

The "sandwich" technique, however, can be executed using a clear epoxy glue for small projects where weight and temperature changes will not be critical factors. The Farbigem process begins with a base of ⅛-inch plate glass. To this is added a second layer of ⅜-inch Plexiglass, and, finally, another ⅛-inch layer of plate glass, all glued together to form the strong transparent supporting surface (Fig. 9-7).

Because of its unique flatness and beauty, only imported antique glass is used in the Farbigem process. Variations in surface thickness that may be present with other types of glass would result in an uneven application of glue.

As in the traditional stained-glass method, the process begins with a sketch which is translated into a full-sized cartoon. A

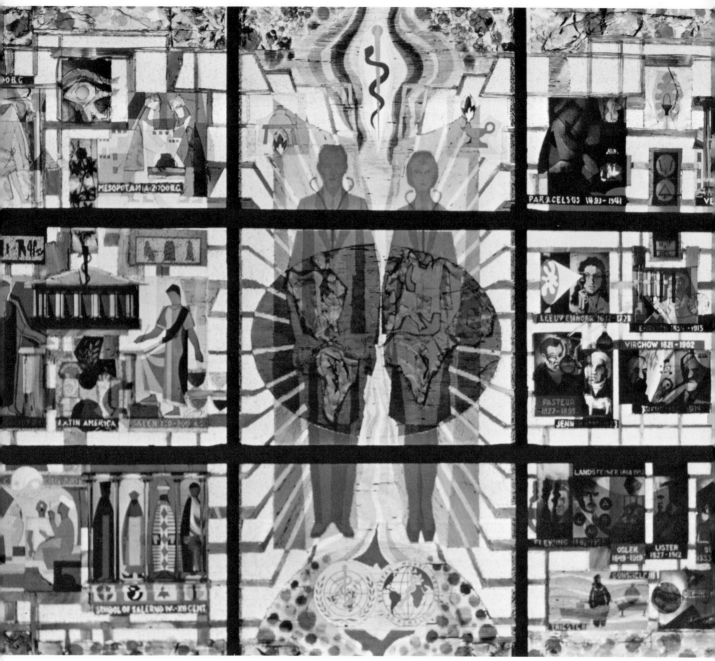

Fig. 9-5. Farbigem glass mural—World History of Medicine, Ohio State University Medical Center.

Fig. 9-6. Farbigem panel.

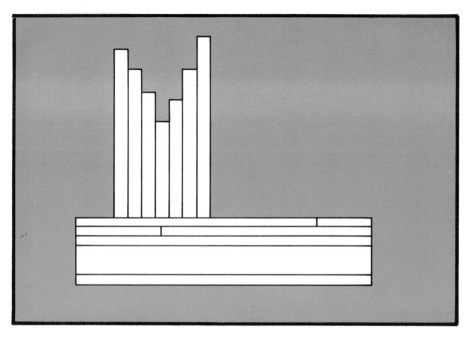

Fig. 9-7. Laminated glass.

tracing is then made from the cartoon to be used as a guide for cutting the color glass laminations.

Cutting multiple pieces of glass to be used on the same surface level requires a great deal of care. No spaces between the glass should be visible to cause an interruption in the design.

Before gluing, the glass surfaces must be cleaned thoroughly with denatured alcohol to remove all traces of dirt or oil.

The inherent beauty of the laminating process is its depth and large variations in the surface relief. Several layers of colored glass are normally used directly over the three layers forming the base to achieve the combination of colors and the depth that would be impossible with only a single piece of glass.

Many kinds of material not ordinarily used in stained glass may be used effectively to build further upon the layers of colored glass. Farbigem uses multiple layers of ¼-inch plate glass fixed vertically to the colored glass surface. Variations in the depth of cut will produce a sculptured effect. Other materials such as marbles, glass rods, faceted glass, and even glass tumblers, have been incorporated into the laminating process.

SOURCES OF SUPPLY

CAME LEAD AND SOLDER

Crown Metal Company
117 East Washington Street
Milwaukee, Wisconsin   53204

Gardiner Metal Company
4820 South Campbell Avenue
Chicago, Illinois   60632

White Metal Rolling and Stamping
  Corporation
80-84 Moultrie Street
Brooklyn, New York   11222

COPPER FOIL

Borden Chemical Company
Mystic Tape Division
1700 Winnetka Street
Northfield, Illinois   60093

EPOXY RESIN

Benesco
40 North Rock Hill Street
St. Louis, Missouri   63119

H & M Plastics Corporation
129 South 2nd Street
Philadelphia, Pennsylvania   19106

Thermoset Plastics, Inc.
5101 East 65th Street
Indianapolis, Indiana   46220

FLUX

Ruby Chemical Company
68 McDowell Street
Columbus, Ohio   43215

GALVANIZED STEEL BARS

Chicago Metallic Sash Company
4901 South Austin Avenue
Chicago, Illinois   60638

White Metal Rolling and Stamping
  Corp.
80-84 Moultrie Street
Brooklyn, New York   11222

GLASS

Advance Glass Company
Grant and Decrow Avenues
Newark, Ohio   43055

S. A. Bendheim Company, Inc.
122 Hudson Street
New York, New York   10013

Bienenfeld Industries, Inc.
1541 Covert Street
Brooklyn, New York   11227

Blenko Glass Company
Milton, West Virginia   25541

Kokomo Opalescent Glass Company
P. O. Box 809
Kokomo, Indiana   46901

The Paul Wismach Glass Company,
  Inc.
Paden City, West Virginia   26159

GLASS CUTTING TOOLS

The Fletcher-Terry Company
Spring Lane
Farmington, Connecticut   06032

Sommer & Maca
5501 West Ogden Avenue
Chicago, Illinois   60650

GLASS JEWELS AND NOVELTIES

S. A. Bendheim Company, Inc.
122 Hudson Street
New York, New York   10013

Whittemore-Durgin Glass Company
Box 2065
Hanover, Massachusetts   02339

GLASS PAINTING SUPPLIES

Aremco Products, Inc.
P. O. Box 145
Briarcliff, New York   10510

Stewart Clay Company
133 Mulberry Street
New York, New York   10013

L. Reusche and Company
2 Lister Avenue
Newark, New Jersey   07105

White Metal Rolling and Stamping
   Corporation
80-84 Moultrie Street
Brooklyn, New York   11222

GREASE AND RELEASE AGENTS

Famous Lubricants
124 West 47th Street
Chicago, Illinois   60609

LAMP AND LIGHTING FIXTURE
   PARTS

Angelo Brothers Company
10981 Decatur Road
Philadelphia, Pennsylvania   19154

J. G. Holzgang Company
3744 South Broadway Place
Los Angeles, California   90007

ZINC CAMES AND CHANNELS

Chicago Metallic Sash Company
4901 South Austin Avenue
Chicago, Illinois   60638

MISCELLANEOUS SUPPLIES

S. Camlott-Lead Cutting Knives
520 Hollywood Avenue
Salt Lake City, Utah   84105

Nitschke Products, Inc.
P. O. Box 104
Oak Park, Illinois   60303

Rainbow Studios
78 South Broadway
Nyack, New York   10960

The Stained Glass Club
482 Tappan Road
Northvale, New Jersey   07647

Whittemore-Durkin Glass Company
Box 2065
Hanover, Massachusetts   02339

BIBLIOGRAPHY

History

Armitage, E. L., *Stained Glass.* Newton, Mass.: Branford, 1960.

Aubert, Marcel, *French Cathedrals.* London: Batsford.

Beyer, Askar, *Kirchenferister.* Hamburg: Friedrich Lometsch-Verlag.

Hauvet, E., *Chartres Cathedral.* Chartres: Durand.

Leymarie, Jean, *Jerusalem Windows of Marc Chagall.* New York: Braziller, 1967.

Marchini, G., *Italian Stained Glass Windows.* New York: Abrams.

Piper, John, *Stained Glass: Art of Anti-Art.* New York: Van Nostrand, 1968.

Reyntiens, Patrick, *Technique of Stained Glass,* New York: Watson-Guptill, 1967.

White, James, and Wynne Michael, *Irish Stained Glass.* Dublin: Giel & Son.

Witzbeben, J., *Stained Glass in French Cathedrals.* New York: Reynal.

Technique

Armitage, E. L. *Stained Glass.* Newton, Mass.: Branford, 1960.

Harries, John. *Stained Glass.* International Publications Service, 1968.

Kraft, Eva Frodl. *Stained Glass: History and Technique.* New York: McGraw-Hill, 1973.

Labino, Dominick. *Visual Art in Glass.* Dubuque: William C. Brown, 1968.

Lee, Lawrence. *Stained Glass.* New York: Oxford University Press, 1967.

Lips, Claude. *Art and Stained Glass.* Garden City, N.Y.: Doubleday, 1973.

Metcalf, Robert and Gertrude. *Making Stained Glass.* New York: McGraw-Hill, 1973.

Piper, John. *Stained Glass: Art of Anti-Art.* New York: Van Nostrand, 1968.

Reytiens, Patrick. *Technique of Stained Glass.* New York: Watson-Guptill, 1967.

Sowers, Robert. *Language of Stained Glass.* New York Universe, 1972.

INDEX

		DATE DUE		

DATE DUE
